the language report

the language report

Susie Dent

OXFORD
UNIVERSITY PRESS

OXFORD
UNIVERSITY PRESS

Great Clarendon Street, Oxford OX2 6DP

Oxford University Press is a department of the University of Oxford.
It furthers the University's objective of excellence in research, scholarship,
and education by publishing worldwide in

Oxford New York

Auckland Bangkok Buenos Aires Cape Town
Chennai Dar es Salaam Delhi Hong Kong Istanbul Karachi
Kolkata Kuala Lumpur Madrid Melbourne Mexico City Mumbai Nairobi
São Paulo Shanghai Taipei Tokyo Toronto

Oxford is a registered trade mark of Oxford University Press
in the UK and in certain other countries

Published in the United States
by Oxford University Press Inc., New York

Database right Oxford University Press (maker)
First published 2003

British Library Cataloguing in Publication Data
Data available

Library of Congress Cataloging in Publication Data
Data available
ISBN 0-19-860860-8

01

Printed in Great Britain by
Clays Ltd. Bungay, Suffolk

Contents

Acknowledgements

An enormous number of people have helped me on this project, which is first and foremost a record of the evidence collected by Oxford's language monitoring programme. Special thanks are due to Michael Proffitt's team at the *Oxford English Dictionary*, and in particular Graeme Diamond for his detailed comments on the typescript; to Peter Gilliver for his advice on historical vocabulary; and to Angus Stevenson, whose observations on grammar and usage trends were much needed and appreciated.

Andrew Delahunty graciously allowed me to use the fruits of long research on nicknames. Paul McFedries is the originator of much of the material on *Seinfeld*, and his compulsive database at wordspy.com was an invaluable source of words and citations, surpassed only by James McCracken who helped beyond the call of duty and who suggested the best chapter title of the book in 'I'm a Celebrity. Get me In the Dictionary'. The sections on World English were greatly improved by material provided by Bruce Moore and Katherine Barber. Clive Upton was an essential and inspiring help on the pronunciation sections, and Mr Swallow's English classes at Hengrove School, Bristol, contributed an intriguing collection of new teen slang straight from the horse's mouth. On the publishing side, Nick Clarke, Sarah McNamee, Paul Saunders, and, particularly, Judy Pearsall, were all endlessly flexible allies during the project.

Finally, special thanks are due to four people: to Catherine Soanes for her excellent advice on all aspects of language; to Erin McKean for her reality checks and boundless humour and wisdom; to Elizabeth Knowles for her constant support and enthusiasm, and her astoundingly wide expertise; and to John Ayto, who read everything and suggested much-needed changes with characteristic honesty and humour.

SD.

Introduction

> ❝ If you want to tell the untold stories, if you want to give voice to the voiceless, you've got to find a language … Use the wrong language, and you're dumb and blind. ❞
>
> *Salman Rushdie*

IF SALMAN RUSHDIE warns us against using the 'wrong' language, the attempt to find the 'right' one is the focus of much of *the language report*. It shows our efforts to articulate the realities around us by creating new words, and by putting older ones to different use. As a snapshot of our language as we are using it today, the images it presents are as telling of our cultural and social preoccupations as of the state of English itself.

The moment the book describes is already part of the past; many of the words it records will already have been replaced by those which are more eloquent of, and useful for, their new time. And yet at the same time as it moves forward, language is constantly looking back on itself, and neglected or forgotten words take on new resonance as events dictate. Much of the 'new' vocabulary recorded here consists of variations on older words, which have evolved to meet the requirements of our new circumstances.

Many of the words here are, of course, recent creations. One of the key areas in which *the language report* differs from other language reference books is in the immediacy of its content. Its

aim is to be a first charting of current trends, and
so includes many words which are a long way from acquiring
official status in a dictionary, and which have been picked up by
Oxford's continuous language monitoring programme.

The mint-new words of the 21st century paint a fascinating
picture of the issues of our times. Many of the themes of the
1990s have carried on, but new flavours have also begun to
emerge. Some of the new vocabulary trends defining this new
century's beginning are predictable: food, fashion, and the
Internet are all rich ground for neologizing, and the influence
of television scriptwriters continues to grow. Some, however,
inevitably take us by surprise as events take over, and it is these
areas which often expand most rapidly. The events of 9/11 made
the existing terminology for war and terrorism inadequate, and
we needed new ways to express the greatest sense of danger
since the Cold War. Meanwhile, the rise of Internet chat rooms
and text messaging created the need for an immediate and
highly condensed language, and so emoticons and a new system
of abbreviation were born.

Beyond its inevitable focus on new words and the events
they mirror, *the language report* also surveys other forms of
linguistic expression which are equally indicative of their times,
both past and present. Newspaper headlines, advertising
slogans, and television catchphrases are all powerful shorthand
for the world they describe. They succeed in imprinting
themselves on a collective memory in a way that words in an
article or essay rarely do. Crucially too, they have the forum to
do so. When the satirical magazine *Private Eye* accompanied
a picture of former Cabinet member Clare Short with the
strapline 'I'm a Liability, Get me Out of Here', few in Britain
would have failed to appreciate the link between the jungles of
politics and a reality-TV show.

This closeness between fiction and reality runs through much
of *the language report*. The conflict in Iraq in 2003 gave rise to a
whole new lexicon of warfare, much of which looked back to
film and literature, and even computer games, for its point of
reference. The newspaper headline 'Saving Private Jessica',
Tony Blair's quoting of Thornton Wilder to the survivors of 11

September, and the startling image of the Pac-Man game for the capture of Baghdad: all testify to the blurring of the boundaries between reality and its fictional description. When the SARS epidemic struck Toronto in 2003, a doctor speaking from the heart of the crisis looked to a fictional world to articulate his fears: 'What the hell is happening to my hospital? It's starting to resemble the movie *Outbreak*, for God's sake.'

This same overlapping of the real and the fictional can be seen particularly clearly on television, which shapes and directs language just as much as it uses it. Some of the most successful programmes of the last few years, and particularly those from the US, have shown a remarkable level of linguistic awareness. *Buffy the Vampire Slayer*, *The Sopranos*, *Ally McBeal*, and *Seinfeld*, have each used language as a means of characterization and language-play as a foundation for their comedy. Meanwhile, in the US, 2003 saw the placing of an advertisement by a health authority for an interpreter fluent in 'Klingon', the language created for the cult science-fiction series *Star Trek*.

Changes in the behaviour patterns of grammar and usage are perhaps less striking than their equivalent in vocabulary, where a single word can gain momentum in a matter of weeks. If more discreet, they are, however, no less a part of language evolution and are equally vulnerable to social and cultural change. Chat-room grammar, and the semi-permanent status of 'fillers' such as 'innit' and 'like', are as legitimate markers of language change as new terminology in sport or politics. The same is also true of patterns of pronunciation, a subject which can arouse deep emotions in some. The variety of pronunciation across the English-speaking world is vast, and our delivery of words evolves as continuously as the words themselves. So 'uptalking', the manner of speaking which completes every statement with an invisible question mark (question or not), is now an established way of talking for much of the British and American populations, and is even becoming part of the 'standard' pronunciation patterns being taught to learners of English.

the language report can only hope to be a brief and incomplete tour of English as it stood at the time of writing.

None but a tiny few of the words selected – be they idioms or quotations, slogans or nicknames – could have been predicted, and it would be foolish to attempt a guess at the state of the language in ten years' time. What this study of a few of the most prominent showcases for language does suggest, however, is that English is both reliant on us to dictate our needs, and yet curiously relentless in the way it advances. Perhaps sometimes our language is pulling us along in its wake.

SUSIE DENT, 2003.

1.

What Goes Around...
A Hundred Years of New Words

IT IS FASCINATING to look back at the words which were created for their time. By looking at the areas in which language is expanding fastest, we can arrive at a fairly accurate picture of the chief preoccupations of the moment. At the beginning of the last century, these areas of expansion included time, transportation, radio, film, and psychology. Today's coinages reflect a prolific growth in computer and Web terminology, preoccupations with warfare and terrorism, and a renewed public interest in the potential of science, whether in the field of genetics or cosmetic surgery.

A study today of the new lexicon of the 1900s offers up striking examples of the cyclical nature of history and of words. The first decade of the 20th century, which saw the end of the South African Boer War but which retained a sense of social and political unease, introduced the concepts of *pacifism* and *war crime*, *racialism* and *social security*, and of *propaganda* and *pogroms*. The terms *genetics*, *identity card*, *tabloid journalism*, *voyeur*, and *remote control* were all born in that opening decade, but have maintained their places in our language for over 100 years. That is not to say that the first decade of this century is merely a duplication of the last. *Beehive*, *bakelite*, *toodle-oo*, and *floozie* all carry the unmistakable stamp of their times even as they have survived into the present, whilst the 2000s are providing rich evidence of new iconic terms filling the gaps in their new social and technological environment.

Some words did not survive. Of those new coinages of 1903, *marconigraphy* and *Marconism* (two of the unsuccessful candidates in the large group of words for wireless telegraphy), *Mauser* (to shoot with a Mauser rifle), and *automobility*, failed to make any longer-lasting impact. Language is full of such 'fizzlers': of the several candidate names coined around a new idea, only one or two will usually survive.

Below is a further selection of words making the headlines in 1903, set against a number of those making their mark a hundred years on, and some which remain just as relevant today as when they were first coined. Many may startle with their true age.

1903	2003	Then as now
automobility	speed dating	propaganda
divvy	celebreality	chow-mein
fritz	precipice bond	hangover
buffalo	weapons-grade	clone
wireless	Botox® party	identity card
segregation	cyberbegging	solar heating
gratters	therapeutic cloning	multi-racial
Brachiosaurus	dataveillance	tabloid journalism
superman	homebounder	supertax
tin hat	decapitation strike	landfill
Weltpolitik	Lipostructure®	voyeur
Shinola	cruftiness	remote control
	moblogging	

1903

automobility: the use of automobiles or motor vehicles as a mode of locomotion or travel.

divvy: extremely pleasant, 'divine', 'heavenly'. The word derives from the first syllable of divine.

> *I heard one of them say that 'the dimpy was divvy', and this, when translated, meant that a certain dinner party was divine.*
> – Daily Chronicle, 1903.

fritz: The US slang phrase *on the fritz* meant 'out of order, defective, unsatisfactory', while *to put on the fritz* meant 'to spoil or destroy'.

buffalo: to overpower, overawe, or constrain by superior force or influence; to outwit, perplex.

> *Buffaloed – Bluffed.* — Headline in the *Cincinnati Enquirer*, 1903, on Boston winning the first baseball World Series thanks to the techniques of baseman Jimmy Collins from Buffalo.

wireless: the transmission of speech and other uncoded signals by means of radio waves. The word *wireless* originated earlier but simply meant 'without wires', as in *wireless telegraphy* (1894).

> *First in this great field of making the 'wireless' a handmaid of commerce is the de Forrest system, which has won the approval also of the United States government.* — New York Commercial Advertiser, 1903.

segregation: the enforced separation of different racial groups in a country or community.

> *The Afro-American people have been held together rather by the segregation decreed by law ... than by ties of co-sanguinity.*
> – T. T. Fortune, 1903.

gratters or **congratters:** a colloquial term at school and university for 'congratulations'.

> *'Gratters, Sandford,' he said, 'on your rowing to-day.'*
> – D. Coke, *Sandford of Merton*, 1903.

Brachiosaurus: A genus of huge dinosaurs, with forelegs longer than the hind legs. The name comes from the two Greek words meaning 'arm' and 'lizard'.

> *The term 'Brachiosaurus altithorax' is therefore proposed in recognition of the great size and unusually long humerus of this specimen.* – E. S. Riggs in the *American Journal of Science*, 1903.

superman: an ideal superior man (*Übermensch*), conceived by Nietzsche in his work *Thus Spake Zarathustra* as being evolved from the normal human type. It is used figuratively to describe a man of extraordinary power or ability, a superior being.

tin hat: a metal hat or helmet, worn for protection against shrapnel.

> *A Tommy in a tin hat as I squared with a couple o' blow.*
> – A. M. Binstead, *Pitcher in Paradise*, 1903

Weltpolitik: world affairs from a political standpoint; a particular country's policy towards the world at large.

> *Lord George Hamilton said … that the one thing needed to make the U.S.A. friends with us was their going into Weltpolitik.*
> – J. Bailey, *Diary*, 1903.

Shinola: a proprietary name for a brand of boot polish. The term was later used figuratively and in the colloquial phrases *not to know shit from Shinola,* denoting ignorance or innocence, and *neither shit nor Shinola,* neither one thing nor the other. The *Oxford English Dictionary* quotes a 1930s rhyme *There was a young man from Arcola, who didn't know shit from Shinola.*

2003

speed dating: a form of dating in which a man or woman talks to a series of prospective partners in rotation and for three minutes only.

> *Not everyone was on planet bliss; one girl got up after three seconds' conversation, saying, 'I'm sorry, I've had enough.' Perhaps she had just refined the concept of speed-dating to dizzying new velocity.* – *The Independent*, February 2003.

celebreality: a TV format which shows celebrities in real-life situations.

> *Celebreality, the junk genre du jour, turns the notion of reality TV upside down.* – New York Times, January 2003.

precipice bond: a bond which offers high income potential but which is also high-risk.

> *The Financial Ombudsman Service . . . has received 2,500 complaints about 'precipice bonds' which are nearing maturity with massive losses.* – Daily Telegraph, May 2003.

weapons-grade: an extreme version of something. This sense is a development from the original meaning of fissionable material, such as weapons-grade plutonium.

> *Weapons-grade has been used to modify everything from a Toyota's torque output to Elvis Presley's charisma.*
> – New York Times Magazine, May 2003.

Botox® party: a party where participants are injected with low levels of Botox®, a form of botulism which can freeze facial wrinkles and which became a particularly popular form of anti-ageing treatment in the 1990s.

cyberbegging: the soliciting of money on a website. The term is also known as **e-panhandling** by some search engines.

therapeutic cloning: a form of stem cell therapy whereby copies of healthy human cells are made for use in transplants or for the repair of damaged tissues and organs in other patients.

> *For the immediate future, Congress would be wise to ban reproductive cloning as far too risky while allowing therapeutic cloning to proceed.* – New York Times, January 2003.

dataveillance: the action of monitoring personal behaviour through the study of a data trail.

homebounder: a young person who cannot afford to buy a first home and so is forced to live at home with their parents. This term compares with another, *boomerang kid*, a child who returns home for the same reason.

decapitation strike: a military strike designed to kill or overthrow the enemy's leader. The term became prominent during the early days of the 2003 Iraq conflict, when it was used in reference to attempts to overthrow Saddam Hussein.

> *US unsure if heads rolled in decapitation strike.* – Headline from *ABC News Online*, March 2003.

Lipostructure®: a technique in cosmetic surgery whereby a patient's own body fat is transferred to reshape and correct other parts of their body. The term is perhaps the next linguistic stage on from *liposuction,* which was coined in 1983.

cruftiness: the quality of being shoddy, ugly, or redundant, and a term used particularly of computer configurations.

moblogging: mobile web-logging – the writing of Internet diaries and accounts whilst on the move.

> *There have been suggestions that during a conflict the Internet could now be used by 'moblogging' journalists, who could now, in theory, upload photos and video from the frontline direct to the net* – The Guardian, February 2003.

JUST HOW MANY NEW WORDS ARE THERE?

We shall never know just how many words were coined in the 20th century, but the English language has grown enormously over those 100 years. The *Oxford English Dictionary* records approximately 90,000 new words and new meanings of old words which came into the language in that time. In other words, each year on average 900 neologisms have made a sufficient mark as to be established in the language.

2.

In the Spotlight: The Words in the News

❝ We should need new words. The old ones just would not fit. ❞

J. L. Austin, English philosopher

IN THE 2000s (or the *noughties*, *oughties*, or *zips*), a newly-minted word has an unprecedented opportunity to be heard beyond its original speaker. With 24-hour TV and news coverage, and the infinite space of the Internet, the chain of ears and mouths has never been longer, and the repetition of a new word today takes a fraction of the time it would have taken a hundred years ago.

Only the smallest percentage of new words make it into a dictionary. Words are servants of events, and those words which prove ephemeral are quickly replaced by coinages more relevant to their time. Sometimes, however, new expressions are given more than one opportunity to take root, and those which are superseded may yet return: a very recent word such as *superinfector*, coined just weeks after the World Health Organization issued its first warning about the SARS epidemic in 2003, will almost certainly be needed again. The rather clumsy initialism MVVD however – *Male Vertical Volume Drinker* – may not stand the test of time.

Looking at new words allows us to get a glimpse of lexical change in progress. Below are just a few of the neologisms which have been capturing our attention and which lexicographers are monitoring closely for staying power. How many of them will last and make it into a dictionary is anyone's guess but is also, in a curious way, up to us. If some of them do quickly disappear, they nonetheless speak volumes about the time and place in which they were created.

apple z: to undo. To hit the keys 'apple' and 'z' on a computer is to undo the last command.

appointment television: television programmes which a viewer sets aside time to watch.

awfulize: to think negatively, even about relatively benign events.

> *'Try not to "awfulize" smells', suggests Elkin. 'Say to yourself: "I don't like it, but I can handle it"', he suggests. After all, it would be worse to let one bad smell ruin your whole day.*
> *– Cosmopolitan, New York 2003.*

clientized (or **clientised**): in sympathy with one's customers or subject.

> *It looks fantastically democratic but even the most skilled journalists risk becoming, in the jargon, 'clientised': coming to share the fear, excitement and eventually triumphalism of the troops beside them. – The Guardian, 2003.*

clog: to take a picture (particularly an uncompromising one) of someone with a mobile phone and subsequently send it to a website. The word is a contraction of *camera* and *log*.

clustered water: superionized water which has alleged healing properties and which is used by top athletes and fitness professionals.

cuddle puddle: a group of people lying together, usually after taking mood-enhancing drugs.

> *A 'Cuddle Puddle' refers to two types of skinship – either a group of people lying together cheerily on the floor (usually after taking ecstasy) or in a communal Jacuzzi. – The Observer, 2003.*

first preventers: the law enforcement or intelligence personnel who are in the best position to prevent a terrorist attack. The expression is a development of *first responders*: people who are first on the scene following a terrorist incident.

Generation XL: children or young adults who are overweight; XL denoting Extra Large.

grey goo: a hypothetical catastrophe feared by some scientists and involving millions of tiny molecular nano-robots replicating themselves and rapidly annihilating life on earth. The nano-robots would use *nanotechnology*, a science which deals in dimensions of less than 100 nanometres or one thousand millionth of a metre.

hatstand: mad. The word originated with the character Roger Irrelevant in the comic *Viz*: 'Roger Irrelevant: he's completely hatstand.'

> '*Upwards at 45 Degrees' pretty much has it all, its two-chord melody deftly phrased, elements of its production hugely arresting, and Copey climaxing with some throat-singing that's hatstand as March hares on poppers.* – Mojo, 2002.

irritable male syndrome: personality changes in men, especially increased anger and irritation caused by drops in testosterone levels. It is an affliction apparently first spotted in Scottish sheep.

lipstick indicator: the use of lipstick sales as a yardstick for measuring economic health. According to some US economists, sales of lipstick go up during a recession.

male crèche: a (facetious) term for a place in a shopping mall where bored male partners can amuse themselves while their partners are shopping.

marmalade dropper: something upsetting, particularly a newspaper article, the idea being that it causes the reader to drop his or her breakfast in surprise. The term is almost exclusively British: the US equivalent, although used less frequently, is **muffin-choker**.

mini-me: a smaller version of someone. Mini-me is a character in the films featuring British super-spy *Austin Powers*. The term **mini-she** is also being used to describe fashion-forward teenage girls.

MVVD: Male Vertical Volume Drinker – a man who drinks straight from the bottle in a bar or pub, standing up.

newzak: trivial news, likened to muzak in its ubiquity.

Permanent news rapidly becomes newzak, a ceaseless, nervous, half-heard wittering noise like old men in public libraries.
– Simon Hoggart in *The Observer*, 2003.

noisy (of a TV programme): much talked-about.

'You have to find something completely different and noisy', says Lloyd Braun, Chairman of the ABC Entertainment Group ...
'I desperately want to go after Saturday nights, but you have to be smart about it'. – *Washington Post*, 2003.

scarlet collar: relating to the sex industry. *Scarlet* is used in the same sense as *scarlet woman*, and *collar* refers back to such phrases as *white collar* and *blue collar* workers.

Scarlet-collar workers are the feminists of the modern age. In the past two years they have moved away from traditional activities such as prostitution and lap dancing to become the majority of cyberporn owners. – Cherry Norton, *Women Take Control of Cyberporn*, 2000.

sex up: to enhance something in order to give it greater appeal or impact. The term was particularly prominent in 2003, when the British government was accused of *sexing up* intelligence reports on Iraq.

It appears that the BBC may have sexed up the reporting of its allegations that the government 'sexed up' its Iraq report last September. But the interpretation may itself be a sexing up of the situation. – *Times Online*, 2003.

skinship: a physical proximity to another person which fosters emotional well-being.

I kangaroo-care Oliver during the day, and when my husband's working nights, for extra skinship we co-sleep.
– *The Observer*, 2003.

SMANKER: Single, Middle-Aged, No Kids. There are many acronyms describing lifestyles: *yuppie* (young urban professional) and *dinky* (double-income, no kids) being perhaps the most enduring.

The classic SMANKER is between 35 and 45. He is a high-earning

but self-centred, narcissistic pleasure-seeker who patronizes fashionable bars and restaurants, sleeps with models ... and indulges himself with expensive clothes and big boys' toys.
— Simon Mills, *Sunday Times Style*, 2003.

stealth parenting: looking after one's children during office hours while pretending to be at a business meeting or other work-related task.

stepwife: the current wife of a woman's ex-husband, or the ex-wife of a woman's current husband.

superinfector: a person with a contagious disease who demonstrates an above-average ability to pass the disease on to others.

In each generation of this expanding network, most of the infected patients apparently recovered without passing on the illness. But a handful, the shrimp salesman, Liu, the 26-year-old and Johnny Chen, became super-infectors. — 'A Single Patient Can Prove Lethal', *Washington Post*, 2003

thumbsucker: a term used by journalists to describe a long article based on complex events. It can also be applied to the writers of such articles themselves.

McEachran did me another favor when he dropped a memo on my desk that said only 'P-E-O-P-L-E.' I'd been writing too many thumbsuckers from my desk and he wanted me to get out and talk to real folks again. — *Pittsburgh Post Gazette*, 2002.

TMI: Text Message Injury (to the hands and fingers, the result of too much texting).

twobicle: a women's toilet cubicle for 2 persons.

Now the Infinity club in Manchester has installed double cubicles or 'twobicles' for female customers. So popular are they that the queues are enormous, even when other, single cubicles are free. — *The Guardian*, 2000.

willy-waving: silly macho behaviour

First impressions are those of an over-enthusiastic designer creating an attention-seeking oddity. A willy-waving exercise, if you like. — *T3*, 1997

3.

The Language Innovators: How New Words Come About

THE HISTORY OF NEW words is largely one of brief brilliance, followed by obscurity. Thousands of words are coined every year, of which only a tiny minority survive. The real indicator of survival is usage, which in turn becomes the qualification for official entry into a dictionary, but much time can elapse between the birth of a word and its appearance in print, and a word – particularly slang – can achieve success as part of oral vocabulary long beforehand. Exactly what makes any given word successful in either medium, however, is harder to pinpoint.

Most of us have a rather romanticized idea of new words, believing them to be entirely new inventions arising from colourful circumstances. In fact, only the smallest percentage of all coinages are mint-new. The vast majority are simply fresh senses of existing words, or combinations and expansions of our historical vocabulary. This makes them no less interesting; it simply underlines the fact that words are part of a continuum, and not entities which develop independently.

Very few new words have a known 'creator' or moment of coinage. Compilers of historical dictionaries, such as the *Oxford English Dictionary*, spend enormous amounts of time tracing the earliest uses and users of words and phrases: very few of them, however, can be confirmed as *the* first use.

Before looking at the influences behind new words, and the factors which can make or break them, it repays to look at the linguistic mechanisms by which they are established in the first place.

'New' new words

Contrary to expectation, completely new words account for less than 1% of all English neologisms. Many are brand names, some technical coinages born out of necessity, and a few the fanciful creations of writers in the style of Lewis Carroll. Unromantically perhaps, the vast majority of words contain elements which will have been long familiar to us.

Combinations

Well over half of all new words are the results of compounding existing words. Examples include *ladyboy* (a transvestite or transsexual in Asia), *mall rat* (a young person who frequents shopping malls to socialize), and *arm candy* (an attractive escort to a party but with whom one is not romantically involved).

As well as whole words combining, parts of words can also be combined with other words. The potential permutations of the following combining forms are almost endless.

-rage: an outburst of hostility.
desk rage, air rage, web rage, trade rage, deck rage

-gate: denoting a scandal (after 'Watergate').
Camillagate, Cheriegate, Monicagate, Campbellgate

-erati: denoting a clique or faction.
Westminsterati, glitterati, belligerati, inconsiderati, jitterati, texterati, chicerati

über-: super, the height of something, from the German.
über-babe, über-British, über-regulator, über-columnist, überhacker

-athon: referring to a long-lasting event or action (from 'marathon').
backslapathon, hiphopathon, orgasmathon, thinkathon, blubathon, slimathon

-ista: denoting a follower or devotee of someone or something (from the Spanish).
Blairista, Clintonista, Portillista, garagista, tequilista, sandalista, feminista

Suffixes and prefixes

These are equally productive in word coining, if a little less striking. The prefix *'un-'*, for example, can be put before any word to denote its opposite – *unscruffy*, *untantrumy*, *unpublish*, *unrevived*, and *unwant* have all appeared in British magazines in the last two years.

Blending

A further phenomenon in the combination of existing words is the 'blending' of parts of words to make a new one. The results make up roughly 5% of all new coinages. Whilst these tend to show less longevity than whole-word combinations, blending is an area which displays some of the greatest ingenuity and inventiveness in new-word creation.

Some new blends

slacktivism: the desire to do something good as long as it involves minimal effort (= *slack* and *activism*).

blipvert: a television advert of a few seconds' duration (= *blip* and *advert*).

bollotics: a combination of nonsense and political correctness (= *bollocks* and *politics*).

brandalism: the defacement of buildings by advertising and brand logos (= *brand* and *vandalism*).

bungaloft: bungalows with lofts, a new desirable of young professionals in the US (= *bungalow* and *loft*).

WAPlash: a backlash against WAP (Wireless Application Protocol) enabled mobile phones (= *WAP* and *backlash*).

flexecutive: a professional who works flexible hours (= *flexible* and *executive*).

touron: a particularly irritating or obnoxious tourist (= *tourist* and *moron*).

Old words, new meanings

Around 15% of new words are old words re-invented. The new sense may supplant the old completely, or may simply become an additional meaning which will be obvious from the context in which it is used. Each of the following words has moved with its times:

portal: an Internet site providing a directory of links to another site.

skimming: the fraudulent copying of credit or debit card details with a card swipe or other device.

chemical: an addictive drug.

fascia: a covering for the front part of a mobile phone.

zipper (chiefly US): a display of news or advertisements which scrolls across an illuminated screen fixed to a building.

edgy: at the forefront of a trend; cutting-edge.

sling (Australia and New Zealand): to pay a bribe or gratuity.

sticky (of a website): attracting long or repeated visits from users.

lush: sexually attractive.

From verb to noun, noun to verb

Although still accounting for a small percentage of new words, the process known as 'conversion', whereby a word moves from one part-of-speech category to another, is on the increase. The noun *embed* acquired great prominence during the Gulf War of 2003. Meaning a journalist who joins military forces in a conflict and reports from the front line, it is notable in its shift from verb to noun.

In the opposite (and more usual) linguistic direction, recent examples of 'verbed nouns' include *to blade* (to rollerblade), *to chef, to credential, to guilt (someone) into (doing something), to version*, and, of course, *to text*.

Acronyms and abbreviations

The shortening of existing words is another means of vocabulary expansion. Three of the greatest influences on informal language in very recent times have been chat rooms, email, and mobile phones, all of which call for concision of vocabulary and effort. The methods of abbreviation familiar from text language are creeping into general use, forming such abbreviations as B2B ('business to business'), 3G (the 'third generation' of mobile phone technology), and such startling examples as 'Sk8er Boi', the title of a recent Avril Lavigne record.

Foreign borrowings

The majority of words used in English today are of foreign origin – from Latin and Greek historically and from almost all the languages in Europe. Approximately 5% of the new words of the 20th century came from abroad, and in this period of linguistic acquisitiveness many of them were from far and exotic corners of the world. In total, over 120 languages are on record as sources of modern-day English vocabulary.

The majority of these 'loan-words' came about as a result of cultural rather than purely linguistic influence, and lifestyle terms are particularly likely to be picked up. Food, martial arts, health remedies and therapies, science, and plants are some of the areas where English is currently assimilating most rapidly. Recent food imports, for example, include **bammy** (from the West Indies, a flat roll or pancake made from cassava flour), **bento** (a Japanese-style packed lunch), **macchiato** (from Italy, espresso coffee with a dash of frothy steamed milk), and **bhuna** (a medium-hot dry curry originating in Bengal).

How are new words tracked?

The use of 'corpora' – vast databases of real and current language – has transformed the description of English in recent years. Lexicographers are now able to study evidence of every word they include in a dictionary: how it is used in spoken and written contexts, and, crucially, how it is evolving. Into corpora are fed newspaper articles, novels, leaflets, letters, as well as transcripts of conversation captured in meetings, interviews, and on radio and television. Taken together, these materials provide objective evidence about the English which most people read, write, speak, and hear every day of their lives, and so form the basis for everything that dictionary compilers are able to say about the language and its behaviour.

This ability to see living language at the touch of a computer key stands in vivid contrast to the techniques used by compilers of the *Oxford English Dictionary* in the 19th century. In its time (the project began in 1857) the *OED* was considered revolutionary in its employment of some 800 readers to capture language as it was actively being used in written texts.

What makes a new word stick?

The British Chancellor of the Exchequer Gordon Brown's five economic tests for entry into the single European currency have a linguistic equivalent. There are five primary contributing factors to the success or failure of a new word: usefulness, user-friendliness, exposure, the durability of the subject it describes, and its potential associations or extensions (we know, for example, that *dot-com* is established when we see *dot-con* or *dot-bomb* in print).

But what counts as new? Some linguists restrict their definition to those words which have taken up permanent residence fifty or so years on from their first use. But this denies the impact of those which prove to be shorter-lived and which nonetheless survive as eloquent records of the event or time which prompted their creation. *Whizz-bangs* (1910s), *flapper* (1920s), *tickety-boo* (1930s), *Bebop* (1940s), and *goggle box* (1950s) would all be disqualified under the fifty-year rule, and yet they remain a colourful shorthand for the periods they define.

Making history

Some of the most striking new words of this century have emerged from dramatic events, saturation coverage of which has imprinted them in public memory. Three terms in particular gained widespread currency overnight: *9/11*, *ground zero*, and *chad*, all relating to significant episodes in American history.

9/11 and ground zero

These two terms were spontaneously generated by the events of September 11, 2001, when the twin towers of the World Trade Center collapsed following a terrorist attack. **9/11**, using the American method of dating, has supplanted **September the eleventh** even in Britain and in the rest of the English-speaking world.

The term **ground zero** was first used in reference to the devastation left by an atomic bomb (particularly to Hiroshima), and specifically to the area directly beneath the explosion. It is difficult now to imagine the use of the term in isolation from the events in New York.

chad

This word became a central part of daily discourse during the American presidential election of 2000. In Florida, most of the counties with contested Election 2000 results used a keypunch voting machine, whereby voters use a little stylus to poke out certain holes on a card to mark who they want to vote for. Chad are the tiny bits of paper left over from punching these cards, and the voting machines only count votes when the chad are pushed cleanly all the way through. Democratic campaigners argued that the Florida ballot was void because some of the chad stuck to the voting cards and prevented the vote-counting machines from recognizing the vote. Numerous recounts were ordered as a result (*The American people have spoken*, quipped Bill Clinton at the time, *but it's going to take a little while to determine exactly what they said*).

A whole taxonomy of the word *chad* – **pregnant chad**, **dimpled chad**, **hanging chad**, **swinging chad** – emerged with far greater speed than the election result. By far the majority of mentions of chad now seem to be in conscious quotation of that specific event.

4.

WAN 2 TLK TXT?

A FEW FACTS:

- The first text message was sent in December 1992, but texting didn't really take hold until the 2000s.
- Text messages are necessarily the most abbreviated form of communication: each message is restricted to an average of 160 characters. Speed is also the aim: like emoticons, many abbreviations originated in newsgroups and chat rooms whose users try to simulate real-time conversation.
- The vocabulary of texting is highly informal and is not yet regarded as standard English. However, a small sign of that possibility came in 2003 when a 13-year-old Scottish schoolgirl wrote an essay entirely in text message shorthand, shocking her teachers. Her essay began: 'My smmr hols wr CWOT. B4, we used 2go2 NY 2C my bro, his GF & thr 3 :-@ kids FTF. ILNY, it's a gr8 plc.' (My summer holidays were a complete waste of time. Before, we used to go to New York to see my brother, his girlfriend and their three screaming kids face to face. I love New York. It's a great place.)
- Text messages will be used to alert top figures in London's financial district, the City, to a major terrorist attack.
- Over 2 million text messages are sent every hour in the UK.
- In 2003 SMS messages overtook cards as the medium of sentiment on Valentine's Day.
- The number of text messages sent on a single day in the UK topped 100 million, on New Year's Day 2003.

AAMOF	as a matter of fact
AFAIK	as far as I know
AND	any day now
BBL	be back later
BCNU	be seeing you
BFN	bye for now
CWOT	complete waste of time
CYA	see ya
CUL8R	see you later
FWIW	for what it's worth
F2F	face to face
GAL	get a life
GR&D	grinning, running, and ducking
HAND	have a nice day
HSIK	how should I know?
HHIS	head hanging in shame
HTH	hope this helps
IANAL	I am not a lawyer, but …
IYKWIM	if you know what I mean
IMO	in my opinion
JK	just kidding
KOTC	kiss on the cheek
LOL	lots of luck/laughing out loud
MUSM	miss you so much
MYOB	mind your own business
NE	any
NE1	anyone
NHOH	never heard of him (or her)
OIC	oh I see
PCM	please call me
POAHF	put on a happy face
POS	parent over shoulder
RME	rolling my eyes
ROTFL	rolling on the floor laughing
SIG2R	sorry, I got to run
STR8	straight
SUP	what's up?
TLK2UL8R	talk to you later
U@	where are you?

WAN2TLK	want to talk?
XLNT	excellent
XOXOX	hugs and kisses
YMMV	your mileage may vary (i.e. your experience may differ)

Emoticonversation

Emoticons have become an essential part of the new SMS shorthand. They originated in the language of email and Usenet newsgroups as a means of conveying tone or emotion in a message, particularly one of a sarcastic and teasing nature which might otherwise seem offensive. New emoticons are being produced all the time: below are a selection of the most established.

:-)	happy (a smiley)
:-))	very happy
:-|	angry
:-(	sad
:'-(	crying
:-V	shouting
:-@	screaming
:-X	my lips are sealed
:-Q	I don't understand
%-)	confused
:-/	sceptical
:-P	I'm sticking my tongue out
X=	fingers crossed
:>	wicked grin
[:-(	frowning
:/	frustrated
:-*	kiss
:-D	laughing
O:-)	angel
:-O	shock or surprise
:-Y	aside comment
b	winking

5.

Words on the Catwalk

TO BE CONSIDERED hip by the world's *frockerati* is not just to wear this year's essential clothes: you must use the right language too. The vocabulary of fashion is not the exclusive property of the catwalk *fashionista*; rather it is the teenagers on the street who are setting the *trickle-up trends* of language as well as dictating our *passion brands*.

We are servants to *style icons* too. The trends set by the personalities of the day, whose haircuts and wardrobes we race to copy, change so rapidly that they require equal versatility in the language used to describe them. In the course of a few years a *Beckham* (in homage to the English footballer David Beckham) has signalled a mullet hairstyle, a Mohican, the sporting of an alice band, a Hoxton Fin or 'fauxhawk' (essentially a short back and sides haircut), and latterly the 'cornrows' of US ghetto culture and gangsta rappers. Even politicians can set a trend. When Conservative Party Chairman Theresa May shocked delegates at a sober party conference in 2001 by wearing leopard-skin kitten heels, sales of the curvy-heeled shoes rocketed.

fashionista: a designer of haute couture, or an avid follower of fashion.

baguette: a slim, rectangular handbag with a short strap.

bandeau: a woman's strapless top formed from a band of fabric fitting around the bust.

butt slogan: a slogan printed on the seat of trousers or skirts.

geek chic: a style which imitates the understated and un-fashion-conscious look of the computer nerd.

bumsters: very low hipsters (trousers which sit on the hips rather than the waist).

combat trousers: loose trousers of hard-wearing cotton with large, patch pockets mid-leg.

anti-grunge: the reaction to the scruffy and loose-layered clothing fashionable in the 1990s.

drunge: midway between the look of a dandy and grunge.

shopgrifting: the practice of buying an item, using it, and then returning it for a full refund.

camikini (also **tankini**): a swimming costume which combines a camisole top with a bikini bottom.

intelligent bra: a bra which can adjust its dimensions to fit its wearer's shape.

stealth branding: the use of subtle rather than ostentatious branding.

vanity sizing: the practice of marking an item of clothing one size lower than in reality, in order to flatter a customer into a purchase.

third wardrobe: a set of clothes which is between business and casual wear.

downgowning: a tactic of choosing unostentatious dresses, said to have been adopted by some stars at the 2003 Oscars ceremony to demonstrate solemnity at a time of war.

VPL: Visible Panty Line.

yummy mummy: a young and attractive mother, often a celebrity.

covert couture: designer-made clothes which are modelled on off-the-rack merchandise.

squoval: a squared-off oval, used as a shape for manicured fingernails.

6.

Plain Cyberspeaking

WHILE THE MEDIA of communication transform themselves on all fronts in the new *attention economy*, Internet, phone and computer technology continue to lead the race in new-word coining. The nature and size of the Web give neologisms the greatest possible chance of catching on, and many *offliners* are left bewildered by a language which is fast infiltrating all aspects of daily life. For those embracing the new technology, the new lexicon is readily adopted. You no longer need to be a *cybergeek* or *yettie* to know your *cookies* from your *worms*, or to share in the latest gossip from *cyberdiarists* as they *blog* the often relentless details of their love, work and emotional lives.

A few years ago, *cyber-* was the prefix of choice among the Internet *digerati*. This may soon be overtaken by newer tags which similarly offer an infinite number of potential combinations. The new prominence of the prefix *geo-*, relating to physical location, reflects the move away from the virtual world of cyberspace – where the user's location in the real world is irrelevant – to a recognition that a location-enhanced web could open up enormous possibilities. As a result, much effort is being put into *geolocation*, a means of identifying where individual net users are in the real world, and into *geosearching*, a way of searching more efficiently online according to real world proximity, for everything from electricians to takeaways.

Acronyms and initialisms are the necessary if sometimes ugly shorthand for many of the new technologies, given their complex and forgettable full names. The following have been quick to settle in spite of their unfriendliness.

GPRS: general packet radio services, a technology for radio transmission of small packets of data, especially between mobile phones and the Internet.

P2P: peer-to-peer, an Internet network that enables a group of users to access and copy files from each other's hard drives.

WAP: wireless application protocol, a set of protocols enabling mobile phones and other radio devices to be connected to the Internet.

ISP: Internet service provider.

DSL: digital subscriber line, a technology for the high-speed transmission of digital information over standard telephone lines.

DDOS: distributed denial of service, referring to the intentional paralysing of a computer network by flooding it with data sent simultaneously from many individual computers.

ASP: application service provider, a company providing Internet access to software applications that would otherwise have to be installed on individual computers.

Below are some of the rather more colourful expressions which are making it in the virtual world.

abandonware: software made by companies that are now out of business.

bleeding edge: the very forefront of technology. Derived from 'leading edge', the idea is that a bleeding edge is so sharp you can cut yourself.

> *'People have done computer-generated people before,' said André Bustanoby, the project's visual effects supervisor. 'We've done it on the movie* Titanic. *But this is taking it to the bleeding edge of technology.'* – New York Times, 2000.

blogging: the increasingly popular phenomenon of writing online diaries or *weblogs*. A keeper of a weblog is known as a *blogger*.

> *So my blogging neighbour's insights were available as soon as they were web-posted, creating a real-time, second level of conversation at the conference, and making my pen and pad look a bit antiquated.* – The Guardian, 2002.

blogrolling (US): the mentioning of other blogs in one's own blog so that they in turn mention you back. The phrase is a play on *logrolling*, a term describing the political process whereby members of Congress make an informal pact to vote for each other's priorities.

Bluetooth®: a standard for the short-range wireless interconnection of mobile phones, computers, and other electronic devices. Its name derives from the 10th-century Viking who united much of Scandinavia.

chatiquette: the newest form of *Netiquette*: good manners on the Internet or, specifically, in a chat room.

> *When first entering a chat room, it is considered proper 'chatiquette' to 'listen' quietly for a few minutes before jumping into the conversation.* – Website Compass, 2001.

chatterbot: a computer program designed to interact with people by simulating human conversation.

clickstream: the series of mouse clicks made by a user while accessing the Internet, especially as monitored to assess a person's interests for marketing purposes.

clickthrough: the volume of visitors to a site.

cybersquatting: the practice of registering names, especially well-known company or brand names, as Internet domains, in the hope of reselling them at a profit.

> *There are 531 more claimants from 52 countries who have filed complaints about 'cybersquatting', including Tina Turner, the rock band Jethro Tull and the estate of the late Jimi Hendrix.*
> — *The Independent*, 2000.

dub-dub-dub: short form of pronouncing the three letters in the abbreviation WWW (World Wide Web).

egosurf: to search the Internet for instances of one's own name or links to one's own Web site. The number of instances determines one **googleshare** (see **google**, below).

geoencryption: the encoding of information in such a way that it can only be unscrambled once the user is in a specific location.

google: to search for a name or thing on a search engine (derived from the proprietary name of the Google® search engine).

ham: a piece of legitimate email that was wrongly filtered as spam by an anti-spam programme.

> *But there are problems with filters, Rennie said, because one person's spam is another person's ham.* — The Associated Press, 2003.

IMing: a contraction of Instant Messaging, a form of communicating over the Internet.

meatspace: the physical world, as opposed to cyberspace or a virtual environment.

loveware: computer software that is distributed freely, whereby the developer asks for users to think kindly of them in lieu of payment.

lurker: a user of Internet chat rooms or newsgroups who does not participate. It is said that most newsgroups have an average of a hundred lurkers for each active 'poster'.

> *The users are as diverse as the net itself. 'Lurkers' read but never send. 'Flamers' are obnoxious correspondents who consistently*

> *violate 'netiquette'. 'Proto-hackers', still in the larval stage*
> *technologically, look up to 'gurus', who understand everything.*
> — *Newsweek*, 1993.

ohnosecond: a moment in which one realizes that one has made an error, typically by pressing the wrong key.

red flag word: a word included in a lexicon held by an Internet service provider and which is automatically rejected by filtering software as being offensive.

screenager: a person in their teens or twenties who has an aptitude for computers and the Internet.

silver surfer: a frequent user of the Internet as a retirement activity.

snert: a participant in an Internet chat room, or an emailer, who acts in a rude, annoying, or juvenile manner. The origin of the phrase is uncertain; one theory is that it is an acronym for 'snot-nosed egotistical rude twit' (or 'teenager').

WAPathy: disillusionment with the Internet access available from WAP phones.

warchalking: the practice of marking a series of symbols on pavements and walls to indicate nearby wireless access, so that other computer users can connect to the Internet wirelessly on their laptops for free.

warez: pirated software made available over the Internet. The term is a respelling of *wares*.

wi-fi: the name for 802.11b, the wireless network standard which enables the downloading of audio, video, and data without the need for cables.

worm: a programme which spreads across networks and infects computer programmes.

yettie: a young person who earns money from a business or activity that involves the Internet: The term is an acronym for 'young entrepreneurial technocrat', on the pattern of *yuppie*.

7.

Fighting Talk: The Language of Battle

❝ You can't say civilization doesn't advance, however, for in every war they kill you in a new way. ❞

Will Rogers, American actor and humorist, 1924

FOR ALL THEIR destruction, wars, paradoxically, seem to have a generative effect on language. Each major war has spawned new vocabulary: World War I produced *shellshocked* and *no man's land*, World War II *Jeep* and *firestorm*, while *brainwash*, *fallout*, and *friendly fire* were the survivors from Korea, the Cold War, and Vietnam respectively. Military jargon became prominent again in 2003, and new lexicons of war were listed in many newspapers and online news sites to help us to decode the language coming at us from every angle, ensuring that we saw and heard more of the war than any other non-combatants before us. Some of the new vocabulary was spread by *embeds*, journalists living the Second Gulf War alongside the military and blurring the distinction between correspondent and warrior. New words had guaranteed exposure and with it the opportunity to cement themselves in our language. Some became part of our consciousness so quickly that they were soon played upon, as in *weapon of mass distraction*, used to describe anything from a Page 3 girl of the British tabloids to the American Super Bowl.

Old words found new resonance too. The definition of a

just war was one of the preoccupations of 2003, but Thomas Aquinas and the Schoolmen discussed the criteria for *justum bellum* in medieval times. Tony Blair described his eleventh hour efforts to secure a UN resolution from fellow Security Council members as *mobile phone diplomacy*, the modern equivalent of the *megaphone diplomacy* described by former British foreign secretary Lord Carrington, and of Henry Kissinger's *shuttle diplomacy*.

If past language was resurrected for the rhetoric of war, the practicalities of battle required new expression. Each war receives a unique operation codename – *Desert Storm, Infinite Justice, Enduring Freedom* – to articulate the specific realities of the conflict, but unofficial signature terms emerge too. If *mother of all battles* became a distillation of the First Gulf War, then *shock and awe* became the phrase for the Second, and a whole new vocabulary of warfare grew up around it.

asymmetrical warfare: warfare involving surprise attacks by small, simply armed groups on a nation armed with modern high-tech weaponry. All guerrilla activity and terrorist attacks fall within this category, including and especially those against the World Trade Center, since which the term has received wide coverage.

> *Welcome to the world of asymmetrical warfare, a place high on the anxiety list of military planners. In the asymmetrical realm, military experts say, a small band of commandos might devastate the United States and leave no clue about who ordered the attack.* – New York Times, February 2001.

axis of evil: those countries whose governments represent a threat to world security according to the US administration: Iraq, Afghanistan, North Korea, Syria, etc.

bushwhack: to engage in guerrilla warfare. According to the *OED*, the first use of the word in this context was in 1864. It comes from *bushwhacker*: someone who clears bushes and shrubs by whacking them down. The term was applied in the US Civil War to guerrillas in backwoods.

fibua: fighting in built-up areas (acronym).

blue-collar warfare: a US marine term for the unglamorous side of warfare, such as foot patrol. A play on the term *blue-collar worker*.

fragging: a term first used in the Vietnam war and signifying the murder of an officer (usually an unpopular one) by his own troops. It comes from *fragmentation grenade*, which was a weapon of choice for such attacks.

decapitation exercise: a mission designed to kill the leadership of a hostile regime, to 'cut the head off the snake', as US officials described the aim of eliminating Saddam Hussein.

just war: a war that is deemed to be morally or theologically justifiable.

> *The Vatican on Just Wars . . . continued to talk about the need to make sure Osama bin Laden was guilty in the attacks on New York and Washington. The whole back-and-forth leaves Church conservatives . . . grousing that 1,500 years after St. Augustine came up with the . . . just-war theory, Vatican officials ought to have their story straight. — New York Times, 2001.*

HEAT: High-Explosive Anti-Tank (acronym applied to ammunition rounds).

heavy metal attack: a thrust by tanks and armoured vehicles.

hot contact point: a location where allied troops are being shot at.

Indian country: terrain from which enemy soldiers launch surprise attacks.

coalition of the willing: the US, UK, and other countries who signed up for the war effort.

mouseholing: blowing an entry hole in a wall of an enemy building rather than entering via a potentially booby-trapped door.

speed bump: an obstacle in the way of securing a major strategic prize, which slows an advance down but does not stop it.

shock and awe, also called a *Doomsday approach*: the use of large numbers of high-precision weapons intended to defeat the enemy psychologically as well as physically. The concept of *Shock and Awe* was first developed by the Pentagon's National Defense University (NDU) in 1996 as part of the *Rapid Dominance* strategy, and was first put into effect in Afghanistan in 2001, and subsequently in the attacks against Iraq in 2003.

rapid dominance: what the Pentagon planned to follow on from a successful *shock and awe* mission in Iraq.

hearts and minds: those of the Iraqi people; a term used when discussing the importance of winning the Iraqis over to the cause of the coalition forces.

Dust-One: Duty Status Whereabouts Unknown: the term used to describe Private Jessica Lynch, who went missing in action having been captured by the Iraqis in the Gulf War. She was subsequently freed by her colleagues.

moral crusade: a term used by George W. Bush to describe the war against terrorism, and which raised fears in Europe of a 'clash of civilizations'.

killboxes: grid squares into which RAF Tornados fire their laser-guided bombs. A 'hot' killbox contains a specific target which is posing a direct threat to troops.

blue-on-blue: a successor to the euphemism *friendly fire*, describing the accidental killing of allied forces by people on their own side. The term comes from wargaming exercises where the good soldiers are blue and (in a hangover from Cold War days) the bad are red.

mission creep: a gradual shift in objectives during the course of a military campaign, often resulting in an unplanned long-term commitment.

> *Because Phase 2 of the terrorism war is not going to be driven by military battles in a defined theater, the temptation for mission creep to sweep in other enemies is greater.*
> — New York Times, 2002.

Pac-Man: used to refer to troops dug in around Baghdad and recalling the 1980s arcade game *Pac-Man*, in which a big dot races around a maze eating up smaller dots.

WMD: Weapons of Mass Destruction.

regime goons: (also called *dead-enders*) loyalists of the Iraqi regime who knew they had no future post-Saddam.

smart bomb: a computer-guided bomb which is designed to hit exclusively military targets.

> *Strategists tell us almost daily about the so-called smart bombs and mini-nukes which will spare the innocent and target only the guilty.* – New York Review of Books, 2003.

armchair lancers: a term coined by Lieutenant-Colonel Hugh Blackman, of the Royal Scottish Dragoon Guards, to describe anti-war protestors who were 'sniping' at British troops.

embedding: a term used by the US military to describe the attachment of journalists to army units, and their resultant access to the front line of a conflict.

> *Already American journalists are fighting like tigers to join 'the pool', to be 'embedded' in the US military so that they can see the war at first hand – and, of course, be censored.*
> – The Independent, January 2003.

effects-based warfare: the use of force not for its own sake but to achieve specific objectives in defeating an enemy.

fire-and-forget weapon: a missile which is discharged by an aircraft and then locks onto its target while the delivery aircraft can escape.

Tip-fiddle: from the initialism **TPFDL**, or Time-Phased Forces Deployment List. This is the blueprint of a military campaign and details the precise nature and timing of movements.

8.

Talking on Message: The New Political Lexicon

❝ Political language ... is designed to make lies truthful and murder respectable, and to give an appearance of solidity to pure wind. ❞

George Orwell

AFTER THE POLITICAL instability of the last decades of the 20th century, the late 1990s saw in Britain a new optimism in the embracing of a *people's democracy* under *New Labour*. In language, metaphors of reform and rebirth were in abundance, and the use of these modifiers *New* and *people's* – *New Deal, New Britain, the people's lottery, the People's Princess* – was suddenly everywhere. Indeed politics became a major source of new phrase and idiom, with *welfare to work* and *tough love, Euroland* and *the third way* all gaining rapid currency. (The bullishness driving this creativity was, nonetheless, soon undermined, with accusations of *spin doctoring* against the new government replacing those of *sleaze* which had been levelled at the previous one.)

The first three years of the new century saw the mood return to political pessimism, as financial markets tumbled and dramatic divisions of opinion over the Iraq conflict put governments and the United Nations under unprecedented pressure. In the US, the constant threat of recession in the wake of 9/11, and the collapse of several multi-billion corporations, also meant a return to the language of concern rather than celebration. More recently still, accusations of **sexing up** intelligence information, and of producing so-called **dodgy dossiers**, threatened to undermine the Blair government.

As ever, euphemism was a major weapon in the hands of politicians, demonstrating the intricate evasion of the truth perhaps best displayed by Anthony Eden during the Suez Crisis in 1956: 'We are in an armed conflict .... There has been no declaration of war.'

VERBAL CAMOUFLAGE: THE ART OF EUPHEMISM

displaced persons issue: used to describe the problem of Iraqi refugees.

situational obstacle: term for cluster bombs, used in built-up areas to block enemy forces.

unlawful combatants: the US term used in place of *prisoners of war* for suspected militants held in Guantanamo Bay.

restatement of earnings: used by several American corporations in 2002, many of whom were subsequently accused of fraud, to describe corrections to previous financial declarations.

collateral damage: the death of civilians as a by-product of attacks on an enemy.

friendly fire: the accidental firing of weapons in war by one ally on another.

peace enforcement: combat.

growth going backwards: recession (itself a euphemism).

The T word: taxes, used by US politicians.

the physics package: a nuclear warhead.

ethnic cleansing: the attempt to kill or drive out members of a particular ethnic group from a region.

inter-entity boundary: partition; used in the Dayton Agreement drawn up by the warring parties in the former Yugoslavia.

Elsewhere in the political lexicon, jargon showed some sign of giving way to plain speaking, and much of the new vocabulary was the result of conscious word-play, with cynical or humorous intent.

big tent: referring to a political party's policy of permitting or encouraging a broad spectrum of views among its members.

angry white male: a derogatory American term for a politically conservative or anti-liberal white man.

Astroturf (US): referring to a grass-roots campaign that is perceived as artificial.

eurocreep: the gradual acceptance of the euro in European Union countries that have not yet officially adopted it as their national currency.

identity politics: a tendency for people of a particular religion, race, social background, etc., to form exclusive political alliances, moving away from traditional broad-based party politics.

> *Both major parties depend on identity politics. Republicans need rural whites to believe that Democrats are gun-hating, abortion-loving, tax-raising hedonists. Democrats need minority voters to believe that Republicans are program-slashing . . . racists.*
> — *Washington Post*, 2001

economic migrant: a person who travels from one country or area to another in order to improve their standard of living.

prebuttal: a response formulated in anticipation of a criticism; a pre-emptive rebuttal.

> *The White House political team and the lawyers ... were debating whether to steal Starr's thunder by slamming his report in advance – a 'prebuttal' in White House lingo.* — *Vanity Fair*, 1999

ear-buying: the lobbying of parties or individuals for a particular, usually political, cause.

jawboning: an attempt to persuade on moral grounds.

spinmeister: an accomplished or politically powerful spin doctor.

Ms Moore is not an exceptionally wicked woman among a communion of otherwise saintly spinmeisters. – *The Observer*, 2001.

Enronomics: a dubious accounting policy or business strategy, used by Democrats to criticize Republican spending policies in reference to the collapse of the multi-billion dollar corporation Enron, which had issued false accounts.

just-in-time politics: a form of politics in which policies are built around current concerns rather than consistent ideologies.

spinnable: capable of being persuaded by biased information.

S.U.V Democrat: a US politician who talks about environmental concerns but who drives an energy-wasting sports utility vehicle. In the UK, *two-jags Prescott* was the insult levelled at John Prescott, Secretary of State for the Environment, Transport, and the Regions.

pollutician: a politician who supports policies which are hostile to the environment.

unconcede: to retract a concession. The word was coined during the last US presidential election when Al Gore retracted his admission of defeat.

dipstick: to take the measure of someone or something; to take the temperature of a situation.

joined-up government: effective co-ordination between central and local government and government agencies.

Anytown (also **Anytown USA**): any real or fictional place regarded as being typical of American small-town appearance or values.

wiggle room: room to manoeuvre politically, especially when gained by compromise.

9.

Riding the Soundwaves

THE INFLUENCE OF music on language, as on culture, is immense. Whilst new and specific terminology is constantly evolving, areas in general language, such as slang and idiom, are particularly receptive to musical expression. New and frequently ephemeral vocabulary finds its most fertile ground in the young, for whom it is as much a signal of group identity as their choice of music itself.

If there is one overarching process that leads to the creation of new music terms, it is that of agglomeration – the development of a whole chain of words which use the same root. One of the most productive suffixes in music is *-core*. Taken from *hardcore*, a kind of very fast and very loud punk rock, *-core* has been added to numerous musical genres to denote a version that is extreme in some way. It shows up in a whole variety of new descriptions, many of them creative and witty.

emocore (often just **emo**): arty hardcore or rock music with very emotional or introspective lyrics.
grindcore: nonmelodic heavy-metal music with unintelligible lyrics and usually very fast, short songs.
metalcore: hardcore music with significant heavy-metal influences.
fastcore: very fast hardcore.
foxcore: rock music played by women.

▶

loungecore: easy listening 'lounge' music.

slowcore: very slow rock music, usually instrumental.

rapcore: hardcore music with rap influences and lyrical styles.

thrashcore: usually fast-tempo heavy metal music that emphasizes guitar riffs.

deathcore: an extreme style of heavy metal music with morbid lyrics.

sadcore: downbeat rock music with depressing or melancholy lyrics.

horrorcore: music which is either hardcore music incorporating eerie sounds, often samples from horror movies, or rap music with gruesome or death-centred lyrics.

noisecore: experimental hardcore or heavy metal music.

skacore: a musical style combining elements of ska, heavy metal, and punk, among others.

homocore or **queercore:** punk music by and about gays and lesbians.

synthcore (also called **coldwave**): industrial electronic rock music.

mathcore (more often **math rock**): rock music with difficult time signatures.

A contender for the most popular prefix, meanwhile, is *electro-*. *Electro* itself (from *electronic*) is a musical style that blends funk and synthesizers with elements of hip-hop. Examples include **electroclash** (sometimes **electroklash**), electronic dance music inspired by punk, often with an important visual or live-performance element; **electro-pop**, pop music that relies heavily on electronic instruments, especially synthesizers; **electro-grind**, noisy, non-melodic music blending electronic and heavy metal styles; **electro-jazz**, fusion jazz with an emphasis on funky rhythms and synthesizers; **electro-goth**, electronic music with morbid or gothic themes and lyrics, or played by musicians dressed in gothic style, and **electro-tech** or **electro-techno**, electronic music with elements of techno and

house styles. Other *electro-* forms found include **electro-noir,**
electro-baroque, electro-boogie, electro-bossa, electro-
death, electro-dub, and **electro-funk,** and the genres,
collectively, are referred to as **electronica** in the US.

There are other recent coinages in music that are both
evocative and interesting.

gabba: very fast-tempo techno music with beats per minute
exceeding 200.

> *As happy hardcore scales the charts and jungle gains widespread*
> *recognition, the northern rave scene continues to pledge undying*
> *allegiance to the impenetrable speedcore of Lowlands gabba.*
> *— i-D*, 1995.

mashup: a piece of music created by combining tracks from two
different pieces of existing music, usually the vocals from one song
and the instrumentals from another.

sampledelica: music that relies heavily or primarily on the
inclusion of quirky or unusual samples (a similar style is called
plunderphonic).

> *Recording artist Ursula 1000 supplies a mix of funky breaks,*
> *block-party beats, touches of sampledelica and zolo, and a whole*
> *lot more. — Time Out New York*, 2002.

mallternative: rock music that purports to be alternative but is
suitable for mass taste.

Nu-metal: modern, streetwise, heavy metal.

teen angstrel: a teen pop singer who affects angst. The suffix
'-strel' is frequently used in music terminology – *popstrel* is another
example.

decknician or **turntablist:** a DJ who is skilled at using turntables
as an instrument.

> *World champion turntablist in mindblowing skillz showcase.*
> *— Muzik*, 1999.

newgrass: bluegrass music for an urban audience.

skronk: dissonance, or music incorporating dissonant sounds.

The rubber rhythm section of Samm Bennett and Ann Rupel provide an R&B slap tickle. For those who dig skronk with their stax. — Wired, 1996.

trancefloor: trance music suitable for dancing.

A nice trance groove that rolls along in fine form, before a euphoric breakdown which holds together well and doesn't go over the top. A winning, big trancefloor tune. — Ministry, 2002.

BUST THIS: A POCKET DECODER OF RAP

ay yo trip = check this out.

to bag up = to have sex.

ballin' = having it all.

bama = a person who dresses badly; a loser (short for Alabama, meaning someone from the country).

be geese = to leave, 'yo we be geese'.

biscuit = 1. gun,

2. behind or bottom.

bling-bling = ostentatious clothing and jewellery ('I'm not going to be out-blinged by Missy' quipped Madonna recently).

to bone = to have sex with.

boo = term of endearment, like 'baby'; 'my boo' means 'my girlfriend/boyfriend'.

boo-yaa = 1. totally fine,

2. impression of the sound of a gun,

3. marijuana,

4. crack cocaine.

bout it = real, not fake.

broady = to take or steal something.

bust this = pay attention.

cadillacing = relaxing, 'chilling'.

catch the vapours = to be caught up in someone else's popularity, hype or glamour.

▶

cheeba = marijuana.

dope = good.

flamboast = to show off by actually flashing material items in the faces of other individuals.

flossing = impressing others through extravagant display, especially with a car.

flow = to rap.

fly = attractive, beautiful.

ghost = out of here, as in 'I'm ghost'. (Also 'I'm Swayze' referring to actor Patrick Swayze's role in the film *Ghost*.)

janky = bad.

lime = gathering of friends and family; 'this lime has no juice' = a dull party.

lina = line of cocaine.

lunch = to act stupidly or crazily

mack = a sexually successful man; to 'mack on' a woman is to flirt with her.

marinate = to chill; hang out.

max = to have great fun.

no diggety = no doubt; no question.

nutt = good sex.

phat = 1. rich; really good,
2. (of a girl) 'plenty of hips and thighs'.

quit icing my grill = stop invading my space.

R.T.D = rough, tough, and dangerous.

sherm = under the influence of drugs.

snow = cocaine.

swangin' = swerving a car back and forth by rapidly turning the steering wheel.

tagging = spray-painting a gang's name on walls.

to turn it out = to have sex.

to vacuum your lungs = to take a really deep smoke.

who's the daddy? = who's the best?

Source: www.rapdict.org

10.

The Language Traders:
Business Speak

I N HIS 1946 ESSAY 'Politics and the English language', George Orwell describes the risk of words becoming instruments 'for concealing or preventing thought rather than expressing it'. Business speak, ad-speak, and management speak are often seen as doing just that: wrapping up the unsavoury or simply uninteresting in terminology which sounds good but which may in fact say little. Such phrases as *low-hanging fruit* and *pushing the peanut forward* aim perhaps at the 'Barnum effect': a term used in psychology (and referring to the US showman renowned for his promotion of sideshow oddities) to describe the tendency to accept certain information as true, even when it is so vague as to be useless.

Some business language, however, does reflect an effort to be creative. Words such as *ideas hamster* and *entreprenerd* are inventive and colourful – the result, an unkind reading might suggest, of an effort by the business community to sound more exciting. Meanwhile, while *re-engineering* and *dot-coms* became the business buzz-words of the 1990s, *downsizing* and *dot-bombs* have become defining terms for the 2000s.

dot-bomb: a failed dot-com company.

> *As the debt built in the dot-com 90s is coming due in the dot-bomb 2000s, we must question whether we own our possessions or they own us.* – New York Times, 2001.

dot-con: a fraudulent dot-com company.

e-lancer: an employee who works from home and communicates by fax, email, and mobile phone.

ideas hamster: someone who runs energetically on the **inspiration treadmill**, as a hamster does on its wheel.

blamestorming: group discussion to assign or determine blame.

360° performance review: evaluation of an employee's performance using comments from peers, subordinates, and superiors.

entreprenerd: a computer company entrepreneur.

Enron (as a verb): to mislead by giving false financial information.

> *Senate Democratic Majority Leader Tom Daschle, asked about the federal budget and dwindling surplus, responded that he did not want to 'Enron' the American people.* – Reuters, Washington, 2003.

road warrior (US): a person who travels frequently as part of their job and does much work while travelling.

New York minute: a very short time; a moment.

vulture fund: a company which waits for a commercially attractive enterprise to near collapse, and then swoops to take it over.

booster shot: a favourable report around the time company managers become eligible to sell shares.

> *The rules are an effort to stop so-called booster shots, or research reports or ratings upgrades that could help a stock rise around the period of a lockup expiration.* – Wall Street Journal, 2002

downsizer: a company which reduces its level of staff.

> *Among the tips for these beginning downsizers are 'never fire on a Friday' (because the firee will stew all weekend and sue on Monday).* – Tucson Weekly, 2001

dumbsizing: reducing the size of a company's workforce to the extent that it becomes commercially unviable.

intrapreneur: an entrepreneur operating within an organization and developing its capabilities or resources.

big mac index: an index invented by the British publication *The Economist* which uses the price of a McDonald's Big Mac®, converted into dollars, as a yardstick against which to measure major world currencies.

Prairie-dogging and duvet days

Meanwhile employees enjoy their own lexicon, often ironic and suggesting the occasional use of euphemism as revenge.

watercooler moment: a controversial or exciting segment in a television show which is designed to get people talking about it the next day around the office watercooler.

> *We spent three or four hours very late one night talking about how a programme can basically market itself. This involved establishing one or two 'watercooler moments' which would get people talking the next day.* – Simon Garfield in *The Observer*, 2001

exit memo: a memo, often sentimental or bitter, written by a departing employee to others in the company.

duvet day: an employee's entitlement to an unplanned day off if they are too tired or jaded to work. The originator of the duvet day concept was a British PR firm named *August One Communications*; the idea took off once the term hit the headlines.

dilbert: to make an employee cynical about their work-place. The term is taken from the eponymous main character of the Dilbert comic strip.

> *I've been Dilberted again. The old man revised the specs for the fourth time this week.* – *Washington Post*, 1996.

golden bungee: a lucrative package paid to an executive for leaving the company; an extension of *golden handshake*, *golden hello*, and *golden parachute*.

lifestyle office: an office adapted to suit the lifestyle needs of its employees, by providing a gym or bar for example.

boomerang worker: a worker who returns to his or her previous company on a contract or casual basis.

flexecutive: an executive or other high-level employee who has flexible hours and can choose to work in any location.

open collar worker: a person who works from home.

prairie-dog: to look over the wall of an office cubicle to observe co-workers. Real prairie-dogs post sentinels to guard their colony.

LINGUISTIC SIDE-STEPPING: THE NEW BUSINESS IDIOMS

ahead of the curve: ahead of the game.

getting buy-in: getting agreement.

out-of-the-box: challenging conventional thinking by breaking out of old modes and mindsets.

push the peanut forward: to make a difference. The idiom may originate from a game in which each player has to push a peanut with their nose.

fishing where the fish swim: adopting down-to-earth policies.

low-hanging fruit: easily reached targets. The phrase has echoes of the term *to cherry-pick*.

return on talent: the benefit to a company of hiring and retaining high-calibre employees.

pave racoon paths: to waste money on pointless projects.

torpedo: an incompetent employee who leaves a company to work for a competitor, sometimes after encouragement.

undertime: a play on overtime, this is work paid for but not worked, such as time away from the office for lunch or other non-work-related activities.

plug-and-play: denoting an employee who needs little or no training and so can hit the ground running; a twist on plug-and-play, ready-to-go computer technology.

throw it over the wall: to pass a problem on to another individual or department without consulting them.

11.

The Word on the Pitch: Sporting Language

THE COLUMNIST Kevin Mitchell once described the utterances of football players after a game as 'incomprehensible clarification'. 'The thing is', he wrote in 2001, 'the people who really understand the language of sport, who can read between all the lines of nonsense, are those who pay at the gate. They know it's pretty much all flannel, that what really matters happens on the pitch'. Perhaps this concentration on the game rather than its description is why new coinages in football appear to take longer to seed than in other fields. Many commentators including Mitchell point out the conservative language used by football players and managers after a game, when they follow an apparently unspoken edict to avoid controversy and to stay close to such clichés as *sick as a parrot, over the moon*, and *the boy done good*.

Whatever the reason, terminologies in football, and indeed in the whole of sport, tend to remain fairly constant. It is, of course, the exceptions which interest. The following words, a slightly eclectic mix from a wide spectrum of sports and contexts, are all featuring strongly in the 21st century. Alongside them we also see the grammar of sport changing. One phenomenon of current match-speak is the use of a special 'sports perfect' tense to describe, retrospectively, an incident in a game, as in *Beckham has run down the line and crossed into the box, and Scholes has just headed it into the far corner*.

Ham and egging: when different team members perform well at different times to produce a good overall result.

> *Michael Jordan has used several analogies to describe what he and Scottie Pippen can do to an opponent when both are at the top of their game. His favorite is 'ham-and-egging,' when one or the other comes out strong and one or the other finishes strong.*
> — *Chicago Tribune*, April 11, 1997

onion bag: a goal net. The term is used particularly for scoring a goal in football (*he's put it in the onion bag*).

gene doping: modifying a person's genetic makeup so that the body produces more hormones or other natural substances that improve athletic performance.

> *But in an era when some athletes are willing to risk everything, including their health, for a shot at a gold medal, the gene dopers can't be far behind.* — *Wall Street Journal*, 2000.

handbags: a minor spat over something trivial on a sports pitch (with obvious sexist connotations).

clogger: a footballer who habitually fouls when tackling someone. The *Oxford English Dictionary* suggests that the word could derive from the sense of the verb *to clog*, meaning to obstruct, hinder, (literally to put clogs on someone), or to 'perform a clog dance'.

Route One: in football, the use of a long kick upfield as an attacking tactic. The term comes from a phrase used in the 1960s television show *Quizball*, in which questions led to scoring a goal, *Route One* being a direct path.

racino: a horse racing track that also includes slot machines, video gambling terminals, or other casino features.

catenaccio: a defensive form of play in football, especially one employing a sweeper. The word originates in the Italian *catena*, meaning a bolt or chain.

greys on trays: older adult snowboarders.

a big ask: a tough challenge, originally applied to cricket teams and now often used in reference to football also. The phrase comes from Australia but is now frequently used in the UK. Other terms following the same pattern are a **big get**, which is a successful outcome to the challenge of the **big ask**, and a **big out**, which describes an injured or suspended player who is a loss to the team.

tonk: to defeat heavily. The word is imitative of the sound of a powerful blow reaching its target.

> *OK, so the reality is that you will probably be soundly tonked by a bunch of Italian stallions who play football with a flair and sophistication you never possessed – even in your prime.*
> – XL for Men, 1997.

early doors: early on, especially in a game or contest. Although not a new term – it apparently originated as a reference to admission to a music hall some time before the start of the per-formance – it is one of the hallmark phrases of the commentator Ron Atkinson and is frequently used in football commentary.

> *I've summoned the team in early doors today, and I can tell that some of them arenae too chuffed.* – Irvine Welsh, Filth, 1998.

silver goal: This replaced the golden goal in European competition in May 2003. Unlike the golden goal, whereby a team which scores a goal in extra time immediately wins the match, the silver goal rule means that the half of extra time will be played to the full.

nutmeg: to kick the ball through an opposing player's legs. *Nutmegs* are a now obsolete slang term for a man's testicles.

> *There are times when West Ham – with a back-heel here, an attempted nutmeg there – resemble a circus troupe rather than a football team.* – The Times, 2001.

lollipop: a flashy trick, derived apparently from rhyming slang *lollipop stick*.

> *In Atko's world, a player who has done well gets a 'spotter's badge', a fierce shot has been 'given the full gun' and step-overs are 'lollipops'.* – BBC Sport Online, 2002.

early bath: what a player goes to when he is sent off, especially in football.

sin-bin: to send a player off a field for a specified amount of time: a 'sin bin' is a penalty box used as a disciplinary measure. The term originally described temporary exclusions in American ice-hockey but is now applied to many other sports.

socks-around-the-ankles: an adjective describing the state of a player who has worked hard throughout a game.

smash-mouth: an aggressive and confrontational style of play.

Twenty/20: a new, fast version of one-day county cricket in which each side bats for only twenty overs. The first Twenty/20 games were played in June 2003.

NEW SPORTS, AND NEW EXTREMES

A growth area, both linguistically and in terms of participant numbers, is that of extreme sports such as these below.

heliskiing: skiing high and dangerous mountain runs only accessible by helicopter.

street luge: travelling downhill while lying down on a skateboard.

canyoning: jumping into a fast-flowing river or waterfall and allowing oneself to be swept away.

BASE jumping: parachuting from fixed points: BASE is an acronym for Buildings, Antenna tower, Span (i.e. bridges), Earth (i.e. cliffs).

zorbing: the sport of rolling down a hill in a giant plastic ball.

powerkiting: using large kites for sports such as mountainboarding and kite surfing, whereby the speed and force of the kite carries the powerkiter along.

scad diving: a sport whereby someone is dropped without a parachute from a height, freefalling into a safety net.

coasteering: the sport of jumping off cliffs into the sea.

off-road skating: a form of inline skating where participants use skates equipped with special wheels to traverse hills and trails.

sandboarding: riding down sand dunes on a sandboard, following the same principle as snowboarding.

helibungee: jumping into the air from a helicopter, secured by a long and flexible rope; **crane bungee** and **bridge bungee** are other sports which run on the same principles.

12.

Quotes of the Century

❝ The surest way to make a monkey out of a man is to quote him. ❞

Robert Benchley, American humorist

JUST AS WORDS offer up a snapshot of the time in which they are created, so a quotation – whether a soundbite or something more considered – can condense the emotion of an event into a useful shorthand for history. For a quotation is not just something that is written or spoken once. It becomes part of our language stock and something which, whether it lasts for a few days or many years, is re-used to remind us of a particular event, or to evoke a context. A quotation is, by its very definition, worth repeating.

Quotations uttered today often carry with them the resonance of the past. Old sentiments become relevant again and we can either rehearse the words of others directly, or re-invent them to match a new reality. In the wake of 11 September, Tony Blair chose to quote from Thornton Wilder's *The Bridge of San Luis Rey*, in which a Franciscan missionary sets out to trace the lives of victims of a bridge collapse who are linked only by their deaths, in an attempt to find meaning in chance and in inexplicable tragedy. 'Even memory is not necessary for love. There is a land of the living and a land of the dead, and the bridge is love.' More controversially, anti-euro campaigners chose to re-write history in giving Rik Mayall the slogan 'Ein Volk, ein Reich, ein Euro' for their cinema ads, a re-working of the Hitlerian line 'Ein Volk, ein Reich, ein Führer'.

The concerns about Europe were rather different in 2003,

when President Chirac denied the UK and US governments the sanction of the United Nations and classified them, rather than their Iraqi targets, as 'les belligérents'. Tony Blair's words at the Labour party conference in the previous spring could have been equally applicable to that political showdown as to the factions in his own party: 'Reformers versus wreckers – that is the battle for this Parliament.' Meanwhile President Bush's apparently unswerving drive towards war recalled the words of another British Prime Minister: Lord Palmerston in 1848 – 'We have no eternal allies and we have no perpetual enemies. Our interests are eternal and perpetual, and those interests it is our duty to follow.' The objectivity of Palmerston's creed stands in contrast to Blair's commitment to 'stand shoulder to shoulder with our American friends'.

Diplomacy broke down in other areas too. Edwina Currie revealed all in her own autobiography whilst lamenting the omission of her name in that of John Major: 'I wasn't even in the index.' Kim Howells, of the UK's Department of Culture, posted a blunt comment on a wall at Tate Britain after viewing the short-list for the Turner prize: 'It is cold, mechanical, conceptual bullshit.' Celebrity bitchiness reached new heights, spurred on by queues of mockumentaries and reality-TV shows. Of fading star Tony Blackburn's success in 'I'm a Celebrity. Get me out of here!', Jack Dee quipped, 'No wonder he won. Two weeks in the wilderness were nothing to him. He is used to it.' Which is positively benevolent in comparison with Joan Rivers on Cher: 'If you want to know what she's going to look like when she's dead, look at her now.'

2002 brought the death of the Queen Mother in a year of otherwise abundant celebration of the monarchy. 'You can shed tears that she is gone, or you can smile because she has lived' was the preface to the Order of Service at the Queen Mother's funeral, while the Queen herself thanked us 'from the bottom of my heart for the love you gave her during her life, and the honour you now give her in death'. She herself meanwhile was fêted at an enormous pop concert in the grounds of Buckingham Palace. 'Not in my garden' was her retort when asked whether she would like the same again the next year.

The quotations of 2003 are inevitably dominated by the themes of war and aggression. Thanks to journalists embedded with troops at the front line we gained unprecedented access to the tragedies and banalities of war. The imperative of supplying continuous news coverage presented them with the same dilemma as that faced a hundred and fifty years before by William Howard Russell, the war correspondent of *The Times*, who wrote to his editor while embedded with the British Army in the Crimea: 'Am I to tell these things, or hold my tongue?' Some looked back to previous conflicts to find the right words for the new one. 'Vietnam Redux' was the term coined by one American columnist to describe the war on Iraq, while George W. Bush's 'axis of evil' echoed Churchill's 'iron curtain' and Reagan's 'Evil empire' of the Cold War days. And, when the statue of Saddam Hussein toppled to the ground, many were reminded of Shelley's Ozymandias, a once great King whose downfall is symbolized by the shattered fragments of a sculpture in his image, found by a traveller in the desert. The legend on the statue's smashed pedestal read: 'My name is Ozymandias, king of kings: look on my works ye Mighty, and despair!'

On the following pages are some of the quotes from recent years which have proved worth the re-telling. Grouped themat-ically, they begin with these preoccupations of politics and war, but finish on some lighter notes.

The Art of the Possible: Political Quotes

With the optimism of *Cool Britannia* fading as the 21st century approached, and in the aftermath of the tortuous US Presidential election of 2000, the British and American people were said to be the most cynical and indifferent electorates ever faced by the leaders of their countries. At 59%, the turnout of voters in the UK in the 2001 general election was the lowest since the First World War, and in a virtual poll American citizens chose the fictional President Jed Bartlet of *The West Wing* for President over the real incumbent of the White House.

With the prospect of war however – what some critics were calling 'Gulf War – The Remake' – electorates were suddenly and dramatically galvanized, and protests of unprecedented size signalled the level of disquiet in both countries and right across the world.

The quotations below endorse Bill Clinton's assertion to the 2002 Labour party conference that 'all politics is a combination of rhetoric and reality'. He could perhaps have added that reality can sometimes take a turn towards fiction, as when George W. Bush commented on the slow weapons inspection process in Iraq with the words 'This looks like the re-run of a bad movie, and I'm not interested in watching it'.

I am Al Gore, and I used to be the next president of the United States of America.

> **Al Gore**, former Vice-President and Democratic candidate for the 2000 US presidential election, who lost after numerous recounts.

You want to fight to the death to keep the minister in charge of our courts system in a full-bottomed wig, 18th-century breeches, women's tights and sitting on the Woolsack rather than running the courts service.

> British Prime Minister **Tony Blair** on Conservative Party leader Iain Duncan Smith's opposition to his attempt to reform the legal system.

On my way here I passed a local cinema and it turned out you were expecting me after all, for the billboards read: The Mummy Returns.

> **Margaret Thatcher**, British Conservative stateswoman, at a Conservative election rally in Plymouth, 2001.

Labour promised it was whiter than white. But it's gone a sludgy grey-pink in the wash.

> Advertising guru **Maurice Saatchi**.

The pages of American newspapers should not read like a scandal sheet.

> US President **George W. Bush**, after the collapse of Enron.

Do not underestimate the determination of a quiet man.

> **Iain Duncan Smith**, *Leader of the Conservative Party since 2001.*

There is only one relationship more revolting than that between John Major and Edwina Currie: that between George Bush and Tony Blair.

> **George Galloway**, *British Labour MP and anti-war campaigner.*

It's now a very good day to get out anything we want to bury. Councillors' expenses?

> *email sent at 14.56pm, 11 September 2001 by **Jo Moore**, former Labour political adviser. The phrase 'a good day to bury bad news' quickly established itself, but was not actually said.*

Our note-takers have trouble with asterisks.

> **Tony Wright**, *Chairman of the Public Administration Committee, to Sir Richard Mottram, who had been reported as saying 'We're all f****d … the whole department's f****d' in the wake of the row over Jo Moore and Martin Sixsmith at the Department of Transport.*

Blair, keep your England and let me keep my Zimbabwe.

> **Robert Mugabe**, *President of Zimbabwe.*

It is not remotely in the government's interests to produce a document with this provenance. To put it in the vernacular it was a complete horlicks.

> **Jack Straw**, *British Secretary of State for Foreign and Commonwealth Affairs, on the dossier on Iraqi weaponry put out by the government in February 2003, and swiftly withdrawn.*

A dignified and dutiful public servant is now dead. He should not be forgotten. To adopt a resonant phrase of the moment, it will be for history to decide whether to forgive.

> *Leader comment in* The Guardian, *on the death of Dr David Kelly in July 2003.*

European Commission statisticians have decided Britain is not an island. We should invite them to walk over and discuss this.

> *Letter to the* Daily Telegraph *from **Bob Wydell** of Oswestry, Shropshire.*

You're thinking of Europe as Germany and France. I don't. I think that's old Europe. If you look at the entire Nato Europe today, the centre of gravity is shifting to the east.

> **Donald Rumsfeld**, *US Defense Secretary from 2001, to journalists who asked him about European hostility to a potential war.*

I have three things I'd like to give whoever gets this job and takes over INS: my best wishes, a bottle of whiskey, and a bullet.

> *US Attorney* **General John Ashcroft** *after the US Immigration and Naturalization Service was taken away from the Department of Justice.*

I am a man of peace and security.

> *Israel's Prime Minister* **Ariel Sharon**, *at a summit to agree on the details of a new 'roadmap to peace' in June 2003.*

I know you are a man of security … I want you to work harder on the peace part … I said you were a man of peace. I want you to know that I took immense crap for that.

> **George W. Bush**'s *reported response to Sharon.*

The Late Unpleasantness: The Quotes of War

'The war has used up words', declared Henry James in the *New York Times* in 1915. The Gulf War of 2003, part of Bush's 'first war of the 21st century' – that against terrorism – seemed to suggest otherwise. The conflict made heroes out of unlikely characters, sometimes in spite of themselves, as in the case of Mohammed Saeed al-Sahaf, the Iraqi Information Minister, who proved to be a master of spin and metaphor. In fact vivid imagery characterized many of the quotations of 2003. The controversial figure George Galloway used the metaphor of 'lions led by donkeys' to describe the soldiers sent to war by the 'wolves' Bush and Blair, a saying which dates back as far as the Boer war in which the British army was described as 'lions led by asses'. The snake or serpent also recurred, notably in al-Sahaf's assertion that the invaders were 'like a snake, and we are going to cut it in pieces'. Finally, the description given by *The Simpsons'* character Groundskeeper Willie of the French as 'cheese-eating surrender monkeys' was, according to *The Times*, the most memorable quote of the war, and one repeated over sixty times in the British Press in the first month of the campaign.

In the face of so much conflict, the voices on both sides of the war/peace axis were loud. 'Let the day-to-day judgments come and go', urged Tony Blair, 'be prepared to be judged by history.' Henry James's words of 1915 had evoked the sobering image of a language exhausted and redundant in the face of the horrors of World War I. It would be interesting to hear his judgement of its condition today. The number of voices heard in response to the Second Gulf War suggests that, in this respect at least, words were not so hard to come by.

We have not found any smoking guns.
> **Hans Blix**, *Swedish diplomat and chief UN weapons inspector, of his team's investigations in Iraq.*

States like these … constitute an axis of evil, arming to threaten the peace of this world.
> **George W. Bush**

President Bush thinks the axis of evil is Iran, Iraq, and North Korea, and the Europeans think it's Donald Rumsfeld, Dick Cheney, and Condi Rice.
> **Thomas L. Friedman**, *columnist for the* NY Times.

The Government is running itself exactly like *The Sopranos*.
> **George Clooney**, *comparing George W. Bush with TV's mafia family.*

This is not the time to falter.
> **Tony Blair** *in a speech to the House of Commons, March 2003.*

We are governed by people who know nothing of soldiering. The ground has never shaken under their boots in an artillery barrage. They have not heard the special sound that a bullet makes when it parts the air above your head. If only they had, we wouldn't be where we are today.
> **Martin Bell**, *former war correspondent and MP.*

We go to liberate not to conquer. We will not fly our flags in their country. We are entering Iraq to free a people and the only flag which will be flown in that ancient land is their own. Show respect for them … if you are ferocious in battle, remember to be magnanimous in victory.

Lt Col. Tim Collins, *Commander of the 1st Battalion of the Royal Irish regiment.*

I intend to join those tomorrow night who will vote against military action now. It is for that reason, and for that reason alone, and with a heavy heart, that I resign from the government.

Robin Cook, *former leader of the House of Commons.*

We live in a time where we have fictitious election results that elect a fictitious president – a man sending us to war for fictitious reasons.

Michael Moore, *film-maker, at his award speech at the 2003 Oscars ceremony.*

The Prime Minister was asked in the House of Commons about Iraq and replied with a satisfied gleam: 'Saddam is in his cage.' What few of us realized at the time was that the self-appointed zookeepers were abrogating to themselves the right to shoot the beast.

Julian Barnes, *English novelist.*

I'm trained for combat. What I've not been trained to do is look over my shoulder to see whether an American is shooting at me.

Lance Corporal Steven Gerrard, *having been injured by a US jet.*

Tony Blair is no longer Prime Minister of Britain, he is the foreign minister of the United States.

Nelson Mandela, *former President of South Africa.*

I do not seek unpopularity as a badge of honour. But sometimes it is the price of leadership and the cost of conviction.

Tony Blair, *British Prime Minister.*

The only land we asked for was enough land to bury our dead.

Colin Powell, *when asked what he thought of America being called 'The Great Satan'.*

9/11: A TURNING POINT

Don't do anything foolish; you won't be hurt. We have more planes. We have other planes.

Hijacker of Flight 11 which crashed into the World Trade Center, heard by air traffic controllers.

The number of casualties will be more than any of us can bear.

Rudolf Giuliani, then Mayor of New York, on the destruction of the World Trade Center, 11 September 2001.

In time, perhaps, we will mark the memory of September 11 in stone and metal, something we can show children as yet unborn to help them understand what happened on this minute and on this day. But for those of us who lived through these events, the only marker we'll ever need is the tick of a clock at the 46th minute of the eighth hour of the 11th day.

George W. Bush, addressing the nation on 11 December 2001.

Whenever possible, remember that you are still free and that there is still beauty in this world. It's OK to smile.

leaflet first distributed by Red Cross volunteers in New York to survivors of 11 September 2001.

It's all yours – just take care of my people.

Rudolf Giuliani, handing over to Michael Bloomberg, his successor as Mayor of New York.

Mesopotamia. Babylon. The Tigris and Euphrates. How many children, in how many classrooms, over how many centuries, have hang-glided through the past, transported on the wings of these words? And now the bombs are falling, incinerating and humiliating that ancient civilization.

Arundhati Roy, novelist.

We're ashamed the President of the United States is from Texas.

Natalie Maines, of the country group, the Dixie Chicks.

The infidels are committing suicide by the hundreds on the gates of Baghdad. As our leader Saddam Hussein said, 'God is grilling their stomachs in hell'.

Mohammed Saeed al-Sahaf, *Iraq's Information Minister during the conflict.*

Please stop sending emails asking if I were for real. Don't believe it? Then don't read it. I am not anybody's propaganda ploy – well, except my own.

Salam Pax, *writer of a weblog recounting events in Iraq.*

Reckless with our government; reckless with his own future, position and place in history. It's extraordinarily reckless.

Clare Short, *Minister for International Development under the Labour government, who later resigned, speaking of Tony Blair.*

I have been reporting from Iraq for six years and I just never imagined it. This is just a breathtaking moment.

Rageh Omaar, *BBC correspondent, on watching the toppling of a statue of Saddam Hussein on the day Baghdad was liberated, 9 April 2003.*

I don't know if they're happy to see us. I think they're happy because they're carting away refrigerators and TVs.

Col John Toolan, *US Marines Colonel, following the US occupation of Baghdad and the ensuing looting.*

The Royals and the Blues

The royal shocks and scandals of the late 20th century gave way in the next to a quieter, more dignified period in Elizabeth II's reign – the result, in part, of a desire by the media to step back in the wake of the death of Diana, Princess of Wales. Drama soon took over again, but this time it was of a different, benign, kind. 2002 was the year of the Queen's Golden Jubilee but also of the death of the Queen Mother, and both events brought a resurgence of support for a monarchy which had looked to be in trouble. An ambitious pop concert, organized by the Prince of Wales and held in the grounds of Buckingham Palace, closed what had in many ways been a remarkable period for the British Royals.

A return to scandal seemed inevitable, and when the former butler to Diana, Princess of Wales, stood trial for theft, the media stood poised for revelations of the royal lifestyle. An unlikely *deus ex machina* emerged in the figure of the Queen herself, who intervened at the eleventh hour. Further accusations, levelled this time against the household of her son Prince Charles, were deflected by a independent enquiry led by his private secretary Sir Michael Peat. Once again, the relationship between the press and the monarchy was under challenge.

The Jubilee girl is here, possums!
> **Barry Humphries**, *Australian entertainer best known for his character of Dame Edna Everage, at the Buckingham Palace pop concert.*

Your Majesty, Mummy.... You have been a beacon of tradition and stability in the midst of profound, sometimes perilous change.
> **Prince Charles** *at the Buckingham Palace pop concert in June 2002, to celebrate the Queen's Golden Jubilee.*

The Queen has come through for me, the lady has come through for me.
> **Paul Burrell**, *former butler to Diana, Princess of Wales, speaking after the Queen's intervention in the trial against him for alleged theft, which led to its collapse.*

Like the sun, she bathed us in her warm glow. Now that the sun has set and the cool of the evening has come, some of the warmth we absorbed is flowing back towards her.
> **George Carey**, *then Archbishop of Canterbury, in his sermon at the funeral of Queen Elizabeth, the Queen Mother.*

It's difficult getting dressed in the dark. I was putting on my tiara when the lights failed.
> **The Queen** *after a power cut during her Jubilee tour of Jamaica.*

Is it me, or are pensioners getting younger these days?

> ***Queen Elizabeth**, **the Queen Mother**, 1900–2002.*

I think one of her deepest secrets is that she finds us all faintly ridiculous.

> ***Robert Lacey**, royal biographer, of the Queen's attitude to the public.*

Don't worry if you never marry. It will save you a lot of vexation.

> ***Princess Margaret**'s last words spoken to Petronella Wyatt.*

Sir Michael Peat must be the shiniest man I have ever seen…. You could have invited the Queen of Romania round to dinner and eaten off him.

> Observer *columnist **David Aaronovitch** on Sir Michael Peat, Prince Charles's private secretary and head of the inquiry into alleged wrong-doings in the royal household.*

The cover may be cream but it's certainly not a whitewash.

> ***Sir Michael Peat**, on his report into misconduct among Prince Charles's staff.*

A Good Walk Spoiled: Quotations from Sport

❝ Golf is a good walk spoiled. ❞

Mark Twain

The sporting calendar of the early 21st century was dominated by the football World Cup of 2002, which saw Brazil collecting their fifth trophy. The build-up to England's appearance was as full of drama as the games themselves, with newspapers devoting enormous space to the matter of the second metatarsal bone of the captain David Beckham (his fractured scaphoid went on to steal the spotlight in 2003). Even the British Prime Minister had something to say on the matter: 'Nothing is more important to England's arrangements for the World Cup than the state of David Beckham's foot.' On the pitch, the tournament provided some genuine drama: against all the odds the USA reached the quarter-finals, while Korea became the first Asian side to reach a World Cup semi-final.

In the US, the 2002 baseball season saw the Anaheim Angels go from mediocre to elite, with some commentators hailing that year's World Series the greatest ever. It was the losing team who provided the bigger story however, thanks to 38-year-old Barry Bonds, who ascended a stage grander than any he had occupied in his 17 seasons of baseball when he led the San Francisco Giants into the stadium. In 2003, Tampa won the Super Bowl football tournament after poaching a new coach from the team they ended up beating, Oakland. Back in the UK, following a rapturous welcome from, it seemed, the entire British nation, it was hard to believe that yachtswoman Ellen MacArthur had finished second in the arduous Vendée Globe Challenge. Applauded too were two Zimbabwean cricketers who dared to sport black armbands of protest during the cricket World Cup of 2003. That was also the year which gave us Alex Ferguson's boot, tossed in anger in the training room and clipping David Beckham near his left eye. The incident launched one of British football's most astonishing sagas, inspiring almost daily headlines predicting the English captain's next signing.

We have enjoyed the last couple of days.
David Beckham, *following England's 5–1 defeat of Germany in 2001.*

You could just as well have put a sports bag in goal … To lose like that on home soil will leave scars for life.
Oliver Kahn, *German goalkeeper, after losing in the same match.*

The last positive thing England did for cricket was invent it.
Ian Chappell, *Australian cricketer.*

I've climbed as high as I can, and it's worth every step of it.
Annika Sorenstam, *first woman golfer to play in a men's PGA event since 1945.*

I hope she misses the cut. Why? Because she doesn't belong out here.
Vijay Singh, *on Annika Sorenstam.*

The hardest part was stepping onto dry land.

> Yachtswoman **Ellen MacArthur** on completing a solo voyage around the world.

We also have a war to fight. The Washington Wizards are trying to make the playoffs. It's pretty much the same thing.

> **Tyronn Lue**, basketball player, in 2003.

After watching yesterday's match, I understand now why all four of my sons are physically incapable of watching a penalty kick. For 10 seconds yesterday, David Beckham was the most important man in the world.

> Journalist **Tom Utley** in the Daily Telegraph, on a penalty kick which decided England's victory over Argentina.

The world will hate it when America wins the World Cup.

> **Daniel Henninger**, writing in the Wall Street Journal.

They are better than us, which is the difference.

> **Sven-Göran Eriksson**, England manager, after England's defeat by Brazil.

All I did was lead them to water. They drank copiously.

> Scottish golfer **Sam Torrance** after his European team won the Ryder Cup in 2002.

We've got so many wider interests … fashion, make-up. I mean, you think, yeah, football's great, and singing's great. But you've got to look at the bigger picture.

> Quote attributed to **Victoria Beckham** in response to continuous questioning over her husband David's move from Manchester United.

My main objective is to be professional but kill him.

> **Mike Tyson** on Lennox Lewis.

If you can keep playing tennis when somebody is shooting a gun down the street, that's concentration. I didn't grow up playing at the country club.

> **Serena Williams**, American tennis player.

We cannot in good conscience take to the field and ignore the fact that millions of our compatriots are starving, unemployed, and oppressed.

> **Andy Flower** and **Henry Olonga,** *Zimbabwean cricketers who wore black armbands at their opening World Cup match in protest at President Mugabe's regime in their homeland.*

It's a freak act of nature. It happens and it's over. It's a freak, it'll never happen again.

> **Sir Alex Ferguson,** *manager of Manchester United, on kicking the boot which cut David Beckham above his left eye.*

Cutting Edge: The Insults

Nowhere are quotes quite so entertaining than in one person's criticism of another. From gentle jibes to career-ruining attacks, the following quotes all show the glorious power of the put-down.

I am a little surprised, not at Mrs Currie's indiscretion, but at a temporary lapse in John Major's taste.

> **Mary Archer**, *British scientist and wife of Jeffrey Archer, on the revelation of John Major's affair with Edwina Currie.*

This Schulz probably grew up taking part in noisy burping contests, after drinking gigantic amounts of beer and gorging himself on fried potatoes.

> **Stefano Stefani**, *Italy's then Under Secretary for Tourism, on a German MEP. He resigned as a result of the protest over his comment.*

Drooping around like a dyspeptic goose in a print frock in the year's dullest film does not deserve best actress.

> **Libby Purves**, *broadcaster and writer, on Nicole Kidman's Oscar for playing Virginia Woolf in* The Hours.

If what you want is charisma, go and find an actor. Actually, you've got an actor at the moment.

> **Iain Duncan Smith**, *British Leader of the Opposition, on the Prime Minister.*

I've met serial killers and professional assassins, and nobody scared me as much as Mrs Thatcher.

> **Ken Livingstone**, Mayor of London.

A long time ago, in an unguarded moment, I used the word 'bastard' to describe my political colleagues. It was a foolish thing to do and I am very contrite. I can only plead that it was completely true.

> **John Major**, British Conservative statesman and former Prime Minister.

It is not well-brought-up behaviour. They missed a good opportunity to keep quiet.

> French President **Jacques Chirac**, on the support given by Central and Eastern European states for the Anglo-American stance on Iraq in 2003.

You have to be clever to turn such little talent into such a successful career.

> **Brenda Swanson**, on fellow actress Liz Hurley.

One looked like an anorexic transvestite, the other was like a cart-horse in a badly-fitting bin liner.

> **Carol Vorderman**, TV presenter, on 'style queens' Trinny Woodall and Susannah Constantine.

The biggest fake orgasm in the history of passionate pretence.

> Journalist **John McEwen** on the Millennium Dome.

A 44-year old woman should never sing in a high-pitched little-girl voice, unless someone is forcing her to do so at gunpoint.

> **Alexis Petridis**, journalist, on Madonna.

Backing into the Limelight

Unlike the last category, where the subject of scrutiny by the stars was anyone but themselves, the following quotes are almost entirely self-reflexive. It is perhaps no surprise that their theme is celebrity, the experience of which appears to be bitter-sweet. Fame and fortune, the singer Madonna tells us emphatically, 'are not what they're cracked up to be'.

I don't drink these days. I'm allergic to alcohol and narcotics
– I break out in handcuffs.

> **Robert Downey Jr**, *actor jailed for substance abuse.*

The longest suicide note in history.

> *Anonymous comment on Michael Jackson's interview with Martin
> Bashir. (The phrase was originally used by MP **Gerald Kaufman** on
> Labour's 1992 election manifesto.)*

Fame is like a big piece of meringue – it's beautiful and you keep
eating it, but it doesn't really fill you up.

> *James Bond actor **Pierce Brosnan**.*

I've never had an ordinary day. To achieve that would be a
milestone.

> *Comedian **Michael Barrymore**.*

I'm ugly and I want the part.

> **Kathy Burke** *on playing Anne of Cleves in a TV series about
> Henry VIII.*

If you're vivacious and a bit wild, they call you mad. That's the thing
about being a woman and successful. If you were a bloke you'd just
be eccentric.

> *Controversial British artist **Tracey Emin**.*

If people in Hollywood don't want to work with actresses over 40,
they are just the stupidest people alive. Not to want me in a movie
because I am 44 is pathetic. I am interesting and fabulous and sexy.

> *Actress **Sharon Stone**.*

Oasis are still the best band as far as I'm concerned. But I'm not
bothered about that kind of stuff anymore. When you've got four
houses and nine cars it doesn't really matter.

> **Noel Gallagher**, *British pop singer.*

I am a moral person, but I think, like most people, my moral values
tend to be pretty fuzzy.

> **Mick Jagger**, *rock star.*

He is really just my baby brother.
> **Paul McCartney** *on the death of George Harrison, 30 November 2001.*

So they is some people who suddenly get loads of money who become very tasteless. How has you two managed to avoid that?
> *British comedian* **Ali G** *interviewing David and Victoria Beckham.*

We worked on the basis that paranoia is the mother of survival.
> **Simone Martel**, *planner of the Michael Douglas/Catherine Zeta-Jones wedding.*

I don't want to talk about us as if we are Shakespeare or Keats. We are just a bunch of spotty blokes.
> **Chris Martin**, *frontman of British band Coldplay.*

I play fairly high stakes, I adhere to the law. I don't play the 'milk money'. I don't put my family at risk, and I don't owe anyone anything.
> **Bill Bennett**, *US conservative activist, on revelations of his extensive gambling.*

I want to succeed in America where, unlike Britain, they do not regard ambition as being the same as eating babies.
> **Eddie Izzard**, *British comedian.*

Foot in Mouth

The novelist Martin Amis once remarked, when speaking about George W. Bush, 'It is terrible to see someone being beaten up by the English language'. Below are some examples of what prompted Amis's lament, together with some instances of misspeaking from others which their creators would no doubt rather forget.

Not that I recall.
> **Michael Jackson**, *when asked in court if he suffered from memory lapses.*

The Plain English Crystal Mark does not apply to this page as the wording has been set by the government.
> *Note on a council tax bill.*

I think that the film *Clueless* was very deep. I think it was deep in the way that it was very light. I think lightness has to come from a very deep place if it's true lightness.

*Actress **Alicia Silverstone**.*

You know the trouble with the French, they don't even have a word for entrepreneur.

***George W. Bush**, probably apocryphal.*

I don't think either he or I didn't tell the truth.

***Alastair Campbell**, when challenged over whether he and Peter Mandelson had lied.*

I have opinions, strong opinions, but I don't always agree with them.

***George W. Bush**, attributed.*

I know what I am. No one else knows who I am. If I was a giraffe and somebody said I was a snake, I'd think, 'No, I'm actually a giraffe'.

*American actor **Richard Gere**.*

There are known knowns. These are things we know that we know. There are known unknowns. That is to say, there are things we know we don't know. But, there are also unknown unknowns. These are things we don't know we don't know.

***Donald Rumsfeld**, US Defense Secretary.*

The public is inching towards the use of kilometres.

***Harriet Harman**, British Solicitor General.*

I would not say he [David Ginola] is the best left winger in the Premiership, but there are none better.

*Football manager and commentator **Ron Atkinson** attributed.*

Entitlement cards will not be compulsory, but everyone will have to have one.

***John Prescott**, Deputy Prime Minister.*

13.

Slanguage on the Streets: The New Urban Slang

ONE OF THE MAIN purposes of slang has always been to keep other people guessing. Language is a powerful demarcator; with it we can draw an effective boundary around ourselves or our group, developing a shared vocabulary which excludes the uninitiated. Using the code of the 'in-crowd' is also a signal from would-be members of the group that they have the credentials to belong. Teenagers in particular map their own linguistic territory – as opposed to that of their parents – with slang. Nowhere is this more true than 'street slang', which moves so quickly and with such dexterity that it achieves its aim of keeping others in the dark.

The last few years have seen a wealth of new coinages, and many dazzle with their creativeness and ingenuity. The majority of words are well established but have been picked up and 'improved on' by a new generation, while some have inverted their meaning completely. The richest sources of the new 'street speak' are, unsurprisingly, music (especially rap and hip-hop), sex, drink, drugs, and money. In all these areas slang changes so fast that only a small proportion of it will ever make it into print. The speed of turnover means that the origin of many terms can only be guessed at; perhaps this is why they tantalize as they do.

Here are a few of the words which have been picked up by Oxford's language-tracking programme over the past few years: who knows how many will survive long enough to become 'official'?

BOOYAKASHA!: THE NEW WORDS OF APPROVAL

animal	dope	minty	rough
bo	gravy	the nuts	savage
choccy	heavy	oudish	skitz
cracker	hectic	rad	spiffin'
crovey	lush	radge	sweet
deep	mesmeric	rinsin'	wiz

Can you talk the talk? A short glossary of teen slang

anchor: an annoying younger sibling who prevents you from going out with your friends.

babyass: a babyish person.

baphead: an idiot.

British shop staff, fed-up with being asked for the latest bangin' tune by Phats and Small, have been trained in teen speak. Young customers in Woolworths stores would tell staff Spice Girls are 'bapheads' and Atomic Kitten are 'mint.' – MX News, 2001.

bessie: best friend. Pronounced 'bezzie'.

Best mates quiz. Find out how well you know your bessie. – Blush magazine, 2002.

bin off: drop out of something.

I resolve not to bin off the girlie weekend shopping spree just so's I can drool over my crush playing footie. – J-17 magazine, 2002.

blonde: silly, stupid.

bootycall: a late-night rendezvous or sexual encounter. 'Booty' is slang for 'buttocks'; *bootylicious* means sexually atractive.

bothered: sarcastic interjection at the end of a sentence, indicating that one doesn't care about something, and similar to 'whatever'.

So she hates me. Bothered!

bowl it around: strut in a macho way.

boyshape: boyfriend.

butters: ugly.

cane: do something to the limit, especially in the contexts of taking drugs or dancing to music.

> *The red LED alerts the user when boost exceeds previously recorded levels – basically, when you're caning it like never before.* – Max Power, 2001.

cotched: chilled out, relaxed.

dingo: cancel, particularly a prospective date.

div: a stupid person.

> *And here be Ridickless, red-nosed and mouthy, with his moth-eaten brains and his tabloid tongue, trapping a punter, sounding off like a div.* – Louis de Bernières, *Sunday Morning at the Centre of the World*.

dub: put someone down with words.

ez (pronounced 'easy'): fine.

fly: cool, attractive.

> *'You look amazing.' He says the words in a perfectly ordinary Home Counties voice and then corrects himself, coughing. 'Fly,' he says, puzzlingly.* – India Knight, *Don't You Want Me?*, 2002.

get hold of someone: have a sexual encounter with someone.

gonk: a stupid person.

gun: attack verbally.

hanky-panky: a boyfriend.

homies: mates. To 'hang with your homies' is to spend time with your friends.

ite: well, hello (from 'all right').

jack: steal something. The word and its sense derive from hijack.

> *The car was found down in Rome Basin.... Appears someone*

jacked it, took it for a joyride, then abandoned it.
– Dennis Lehane, *Mystic River*, 2001.

Johnny no stars: a stupid person. The term comes from the system operated by fast-food chain McDonald's, whereby employees earn stars when they acquire new skills. To have no stars is to have no particular area of expertise.

keener: a derogatory term for a person who is extremely enthusiastic about school work.

large it: enjoy oneself in a lively way with drink or drugs and music.

Not that you'll find Bettany chasing the high life. 'I don't do larging it. Not for any moral reasons, simply because I'm fantastically bad at it.' – *The Times*, 2001.

lashed: drunk.

do one: go away.

Weighed down with a couple of heavy sacks of fruit and veg, we're headed off at the gate. 'You're gonna have to leave that here,' says Mr Security Guard.... We comply. He wanders off. We leg it back, grab the swag and do one. – *Big Issue*, 2000.

lem: someone on their own (shortened from 'lemon').

monged out: under the influence of drink or drugs.

I've done a lot of drugs in my time, but these days if I do a load of charlie or pills on Friday, I'm monged out till about Wednesday and I can't think straight while making a tune. – *Q magazine*, 2002.

muller (also **munter**): an unattractive person.

pants: bad, rubbish. To 'say pants to something' is to bid it good riddance.

Say pants to poverty! – Catchphrase for British Comic Relief campaign, 2001.

pie: a fat person.

poop: rubbish.

Look to the poop – that's the guiding principle of the supermarket tabloid. – *Vanity Fair*, 2002.

pop ya collar: respect yourself.

props: proper respect.

> *Props on bigging up Brooklyn and all, but Tricia Romano lost me when she suggested a local DJ 'booms hip-hop not of the cheesy Jay-Z variety'.* – *Village Voice*, 2001.

random: rather strange, odd.

rents: one's parents.

> *Your 'rents are in a great mood and your siblings are finally not being pains in the butt. Just the peace and quiet you need what with school-stress kicking-in.* – *kidzworld.com*, 2002.

rude: good-looking.

safe: cool.

scab: a thief.

scatty-yatty: an unattractive girl (probably from West Indian slang).

shedded: drunk.

slayer: an assertive girl, coined in allusion to the TV series *Buffy the Vampire Slayer*.

stateful: in a state.

take a chill pill: calm down.

trolleyed/trollied: drunk.

> *''Tis the season to get trolleyed – tra-la-la-la-la, la-la-la-la,' announce the Retro mob.* – *Ministry*, 2002.

swerve: change one's social plans at last minute.

tick: sexually attractive.

trev (usually derogatory): someone who wears only designer clothes and who cares excessively about appearances.

wagwon: what's going on?

wallin': to sit or stand against a wall at a party.

whacked: out of control.

14.

Chewing the Linguistic Scenery: Idioms

T HE WORD 'IDIOM' entered English in the 16th century. It derives ultimately from Greek meaning 'private; peculiar to oneself'. This sense of individuality characterizes many of our most popular idioms, which take their colour from stories which are either known to us, or which, though now lost, still intrigue. A sense of private possession is extended to users of idioms too: we each appropriate our own collection of phrases and make them part of our linguistic repertoire, just as we remember those handed down by parents and grandparents and which featured strongly in our childhood.

An enormous number of the idioms in daily use are many years old, and yet their meanings have remained surprisingly constant. They were popularized, if not directly coined, by the widely-read writers of their times. Cicero gave us 'scraping the bottom of the barrel', Milton 'adding fuel to the fire', Dickens 'apple-pie order', 'before you can say Jack Robinson', 'behind the times', and 'by the same token', while Mark Twain passed on to us 'cutting corners' and 'food for thought'.

Of all sources of idioms today, however, two remain supreme. Firstly, the Bible, and the King James version in particular, is especially productive, thanks in no small part to the translator William Tyndale, from whom it received some of its most memorable turns of phrase. 'The apple of one's eye', 'by the skin of one's teeth', 'to see eye to eye', and 'go the second mile' are all part of its legacy. Secondly there is Shakespeare, who of all idiom-coiners is perhaps the most influential, providing some of the most colourful expressions in current language. 'It's Greek to me' (*Julius Caesar*), 'neither here nor there' (*Othello*), 'a laughing stock' (*The Merry Wives of Windsor*), 'in my mind's eye' (*Hamlet*), and 'in one fell swoop' (*Macbeth*) are a few examples from the vast Shakespearean lexicon of idiomatic language.

In modern times, television is as powerful an influence. Rich sources of new idioms include such programmes as *Buffy the Vampire Slayer* ('riding the mellow'), and *The Sopranos* ('going to the mattresses'). Their effect may not always be ephemeral: the 1970s series *Happy Days* provided one of the most resonant of American idioms in use today: 'jumping the shark'.

JUMP THE SHARK: THE IDIOM OF THE 2000s?

This phrase, which describes a moment when a TV show starts to go downhill after one gimmick too many, is a good example of how language evolves. It was coined by a group of Michigan students in reference to an episode in 1977 of *Happy Days*, in which the central character, the Fonz, leaves his motorcycle behind and takes off on water skis, with which he tries to jump over a shark. From this specific application to television, the students used the phrase to describe other television shows going downhill, or indeed any moment when something good turns bad. 'Jumping the shark' is now used in mainstream journalism, as one of Maureen Dowd's *New York Times* columns shows: '*Clarence Thomas jumped the shark watching pornography, and Ken Starr writing it,*' she writes, adding that '*Hillary Clinton transcends mere jumping. She is the shark.*'
Jon Hein, one of the Michigan students and the creator of Jumptheshark.com, a site listing examples of the turning-points for previously successful television shows, likes to imagine a TV show based on his site. That however, he says, 'is probably when Jump the Shark will jump the shark'.

The following list gives a flavour of other idioms which have gained wider currency in recent times, and which have, or look likely to, put down roots.

give someone the hairy eyeball (US): to stare at someone in a disapproving way, especially with one's eyelids lowered.

> *A gauntlet of bad-ass mohawked punks lined the edge of the stage, giving the band a massive hairy eyeball.*
> – Michael Azzerad, *Our Band Could be Your Life*, 2001.

walk back the cat (US): to reconstruct the events of an operation or event chronologically in order to understand what went wrong. The phrase was probably coined by the author Robert Littell in his novel of that title.

> *He began the long tedious job of walking back the cat on the aborted defection.* – Robert Littell, *The Company*, 2002.

fill one's boots: to have as much of something as you want; to do something to the limit.

go postal (US): to go mad, especially from stress. The phrase originated as a reference to cases in the US of postal employees running amok and shooting colleagues.

> *Just seeing the two of you kissing … I leaned towards the postal, but I trust you.* – *Buffy the Vampire Slayer*, 2002.

to be all fur coat and no knickers: to have an impressive appearance but nothing much behind it to back it up. There are several variations on the same theme, including the idiom **to be all hat and no cattle**.

> *Every dish was all dressed up like a toy poodle at Crufts. This sort of 'fur-coat-and-no-knickers' food not only impresses the critics but seems to be creeping into the home kitchen too.*
> – *Observer Food Monthly*, 2002.

handbags at dawn, also **handbags at 10 paces** (Brit.): minor fisticuffs; an instance of in-fighting and posturing. Both phrases are references to duels which were traditionally fought at dawn.

> *It was almost a case of Prada handbags at dawn as the*

style pack covering London Fashion Week fell out in a very unseemly way. – Mail on Sunday, 1999.

silver bullet: a simple and seemingly magical solution to a problem. According to legend, a silver bullet is the only weapon that can kill a werewolf.

the dog that caught the car: a person who has reached their goal and doesn't know what to do next. A dog hopelessly chasing a passing car would be completely bewildered by success.

It will be very difficult for Central Command to calibrate its war plan to everything taking place in the country now. The dog has caught the car. – Retired Major General Don Shepperd, April 2003.

light in the loafers: homosexual.

Democratic Party Chairman Dick Harpootlian ... told reporters that Graham is 'a little too light in the loafers to fill Strom Thurmond's shoes'. (When Graham cried foul, Harpootlian played dumb and said he did not know the phrase had sexual overtones.) – New Republic, 2002.

kick something into the long grass (Brit.): to defer or postpone something.

have it large, also **give it large** (Brit.): to go out and enjoy yourself, typically with drink or drugs; to give it all you've got.

'You gotta be sorted to get into a club like that.' ... 'Well we'll get 'em in, won't we Kev, cos we're gonna be loved-up DJs.' ... 'We're havin' it large!' said Kevin enthusiastically. – Richard Topping, Kevin and Perry Go Large, 2000.

speak to the hand [cos the face ain't listening] (US): expressing boredom or indifference towards another person.

go commando: to wear no underpants.

Thank goodness he wasn't going commando, that increasingly popular practice where nothing comes between you and your trousers (a government leak would surely take on a whole new meaning). – The Guardian, 2001.

chew the scenery (US): of an actor, to over-act.

Some of the characters are more engaging than others ... But

every player [is] given at least one opportunity to chew the scenery with some furious outburst or tearful revelation.
– Review of *Dancing at the Blue Iguana*, Neil Smith, BBCi *Film Review*, 2002.

salute the judge (Australian) (of a horse): to win a race.

eat your own dog food (US): to use whatever product or service you provide.

like a dog watching television: in the position of doing something one doesn't understand.

'This was my first job in this command and I felt like the dog watching television,' he said. 'I knew there was a lot going on around me. I just didn't know what it was.' – *Macon Telegraph*, February 27, 2003.

drink the Kool-Aid (US): to accept an argument completely or blindly. The phrase originates from the 'Jonestown massacre' in which members of the People's Temple cult committed mass suicide by drinking Kool-Aid, a children's sugary drink, laced with cyanide.

Did the analysts drink the Kool-Aid too?
– *Business2.com*, on recent stock-market collapses.

act the maggot (Irish): to behave in a foolish, playful way.

wave a dead chicken: to make a perfunctory attempt to resolve a problem in the knowledge that it will be futile. The phrase may be an allusion to voodoo rituals.

I'll wave a dead chicken over the source code, but I really think we've run into an OS bug. – R. Rucker et al., *Mondo 2000*.

open the kimono: of a company, to open the accounting books and disclose detailed business information.

Any organization development professional can provide evidence that trust is one of the basic ingredients of a successful company … So, it's about time to open the kimono and reap the benefits. – *Electronic Business Online*, 2001.

15.

Slogans are Forever: the Best of Advertising

❝ Advertising is the most fun you can have with your clothes on. ❞

Jerry Della Femina, American advertising executive

WHAT MAKES AN advertising slogan successful? There's a well-known piece of advice in the world of marketing: 'sell the sizzle, not the steak.' It means to sell the benefits, not the features. Ad agencies talk of the big idea, and of brand different-iation. Most importantly, though, an ad has to be *memorable*. Slogans rely on a number of linguistic devices for their impact; puns, both written and visual, hyperbole, understatement, and alliteration (the 'va-va-voom' of the Renault commercials) can all be powerful aids in the delivery of ideas. The most persuasive taglines pass readily into the common language as catchphrases; some are so successful that they are adapted to all kinds of contexts quite divorced from the product they were intended to sell. 'Where's the Beef?' has gone from a commercial – for the fast-food chain Wendy's – to catchphrase, to cliché.

Advertising which catches a mood and which reacts to highly topical concerns is often likely to succeed. In the wake of 11 September 2001, Ryanair ran full-page advertisements featuring Lord Kitchener with the slogan 'Let's fight back', while a campaign on behalf of the then New York Mayor Rudolf Guiliani carried the theme 'The New York Miracle. Be a part of it'. Such immediate responses might also need to be defensive: in 2003 advertising agencies warned their clients in the UK and US to play down the nationality of their brands as the war in

Iraq fuelled anti-western feeling around the world. McDonald's promptly launched a press campaign in Argentina, where anti-war feeling was running high, showing a Big Mac with the words 'Made in Argentina'. Sometimes a slogan can react to the times unwittingly, as in an advertisement created by the Hong Kong tourist board which carried the line 'Hong Kong takes your breath away'. The choice of words was to prove unfortunate: the ad was aired just as the full extent of the SARS (severe acute respiratory syndrome) epidemic became known, and was promptly pulled.

Political and social causes often generate some of the most striking slogans. In the US, dwindling numbers of recruits have forced nuns to launch unprecedented campaigns in an attempt to enlist more women. One poster sent to college campuses shows a close-up of Michelangelo's 'Creation of Adam' with a mobile telephone placed in God's hand. The slogan reads: 'Do you have a call waiting?' Meanwhile Peta, the anti-fur campaign body, followed up their high-profile protest at a NY fashion show with an advertisement featuring the singer Sophie Ellis Bextor holding up a skinned fox and the blunt slogan 'Here's the rest of your coat'.

2003 was the year in which tobacco advertising in the UK – on billboards, in magazines, and even in most cases on the Internet – was banned, and a rich history of cigarette slogans came to an abrupt end. Alan Milburn, the UK government's then Health Secretary, declared an end to the era by unveiling a new billboard in south London declaring: 'Tobacco advertising – we can live without it. Don't give up giving up.' Meanwhile Silk Cut's last advert featured a corpulent diva in a dress made of their trademark torn purple silk, with the defiant slogan: 'It's not over till the fat lady sings'. In New York City, smoking was banned in all bars and restaurants, leading to whispered directions to 'smokeasies' and reminiscent of 1904 when a woman was arrested for smoking a cigarette in her car. Ten years after that incident had come the first anti-smoking advertising, in the form of a poster carrying the opinion of biologist Davis Starr Jordan: 'The boy who smokes cigarettes need not be anxious about his future; he has none.'

A HISTORY OF CIGARETTE SLOGANS

The Joy Smoke.
Prince Albert pipe tobacco, 1908

It's Toasted!
Lucky Strike, 1916

I'd walk a mile for a Camel.
Camel cigarettes, 1921

As Mild as May.
Marlboro, first introduced as a woman's cigarette, 1924

Not a Cough in a Carload.
Old Gold cigarettes, 1926

Blow some my way.
Chesterfield cigarettes, 1933

Cool as a mountain stream.
Consulate cigarettes, 1960s onwards

For your throat's sake, smoke Craven A's.
Craven A cigarettes

You're never alone with a Strand.
Strand cigarettes, 1960

Happiness is a cigar called Hamlet.
Hamlet cigars, 1960

Come to where the flavor is. Come to Marlboro Country.
First 'Marlboro Country' ad, 1964

You've come a long way, baby.
Virginia Slims, 1970s

Pure Gold.
Benson and Hedges

Slogans we remember

Your country needs you.
Campaign asking men to enlist to fight in the First World War, with the now famous picture of a pointing Lord Kitchener

Say it with flowers.
Society of American florists, 1917

Even your closest friends won't tell you.
Listerine mouthwash, US, 1923

We are the Ovaltineys
Happy girls and boys.
Ovaltine drink, from 1935

A diamond is forever.
De Beers Consolidated Mines, 1940s onwards

Have a break, have a Kit-Kat.
Rowntree's Kit-Kat, from c.1955

Go to work on an egg.
British Egg Marketing Board, from 1957

It's finger-lickin' good.
Kentucky Fried Chicken, from 1952

A Mars a day helps you work, rest and play.
Mars bar, 1965

Sch … you know who.
Schweppes mineral drinks, 1960s

We're number two. We try harder.
Avis Car Rentals, 1962

Put a Tiger in Your Tank.
Esso petrol, 1964

Beanz Meanz Heinz.
Heinz baked beans, c.1967

And all because the lady loves Milk Tray.
Cadbury's Milk Tray chocolates, 1968 onwards

For mash get Smash.
Cadbury's Smash instant mashed potato, 1974 onwards

American Express? That'll do nicely, sir.
American Express credit card, 1970s

It's the real thing.
Coca-Cola, 1970

Heineken refreshes the parts other beers cannot reach.
Heineken lager, 1974 onwards

Naughty but nice.
Dairy Council, promoting fresh cream cakes, in 1978

I liked it so much, I bought the company!
Remington Shavers, 1980, spoken by Victor Kiam

Reach out and touch someone.
American Telephone & Telegraph, 1982

Australians wouldn't give a XXXX for anything else.
Castlemaine lager, 1986 onwards

Be all that you can be.
US army, 1981

'Ello, Tosh, Got a Toshiba?
Toshiba cars, 1984

Reassuringly expensive.
Stella Artois beer, 1984

Vorsprung durch Technik.
'Progress through Technology', Audi cars, from 1986

Free enterprise with every issue.
The Economist

The best part of waking up is Folger's in your cup.
Folger's coffee

The best a man can get.
Gillette razors, 1980s

Just do it.
Nike, 1988

Everybody doesn't like something, but nobody doesn't like Sara Lee.
Sara Lee cakes, 1990s

Hello boys.
Playtex Wonderbra, featuring the model Eva Herzigova's cleavage, 1994

You know when you've been Tangoed.
Tango orange drink, 1994

The future's bright, the future's Orange.
Orange mobile phones, 1996

It's a Skoda. Honest.
Skoda cars, 2000

16.

I'm a Celebrity, Get me in the Dictionary

LANGUAGE, UNLIKE photographs or publicity, is an area which no celebrity, however influential, can dictate. Whilst the evolution of a name into a linguistic shorthand for a particular attribute or style is one of the greatest displays of public recognition, the equations made may not always be complimentary. Nevertheless, if all publicity is good publicity, then a personal place in language may be highly sought-after. To have your name make it into a dictionary and become official, as Delia Smith did in 2002, must count as one of the highest linguistic accolades.

Newspapers are particularly strong forces in the creation and dissemination of this celebrity shorthand, and are endlessly inventive in their choices. The Internet is also powerful, giving voice to the views of millions of individuals who make up the celebrities' public. Below is a small selection of those names which have transcended their owners. The majority are based on the same simple linguistic structure, in which to be the person in question of a particular activity is to be an outstanding example of it, but there are some other identifiable patterns ('to pull a X', 'to do a Y', 'to Z-ize'), which offer a no less vivid and effective semantic short-cut.

■ **Ally McBeal**
The slenderness of the fictional lawyer of the eponymous series *Ally McBeal*, and the actress who played her, Calista Flockhart, has been the focus of much media comment.

Remember when cell phones cost almost as much as a laptop?

> *Now Qualcomm brings you the Ally McBeal of cell phones – the*
> *Thin Phone. It weighs just 4.2 ounces (just a tad more than Ally).*
> *– Wired.com, 2003.*

■ Gordon Brown

The Chancellor of the Exchequer in the present UK government
seems to have influenced the language of fashion as well as that of
the economy. Giving a speech at the Guildhall in London in 1997, and
in the spirit of New Labour, Brown eschewed the traditional dinner
jacket in favour of a lounge suit. Such a suit was known in London as a
Gordon Brown for some time afterwards, and **to Gordon Brown it** is,
simply, to wear casual rather than formal wear.

■ Michael Jordan

The highly successful US basketball player has become emblematic of
excellence in a particular field. To be **the Michael Jordan** of a sport or
profession is to be the ultimate success in it.

> *David Falk, whom one would be tempted to call the Michael*
> *Jordan of sports agents if he weren't Michael Jordan's sports*
> *agent … – New Yorker, 1998.*

■ Elvis Presley

One of the most recent uses of Presley's name is in the phrase **an Elvis
year**, which is a year in which a person or phenomenon peaks in
popularity.

> *The great, searching American anti-ending had its Elvis year in*
> *1974, and those despairing cliff-hangers look even more*
> *astonishing today. – Village Voice, 1998.*

■ Steven Bradbury

Bradbury is the Australian skater who, at the 2002 Olympics, won the
gold medal in the 1000 metres short track speed-skating competition,
being the only competitor left standing after all other finalists fell.
To do a Bradbury is thus to be unlikely winner of a competition.

> *Souths Rabbitohs and North Queensland Cowboys … are*
> *suddenly firming as serious contenders to do a 'Bradbury' and win*
> *the NRL competition should everyone in front of them fall over*
> *under salary cap investigations. – Sydney Morning Herald, 2002.*

■ Tony Blair

The British Prime Minister has a strong linguistic following. A **Blairista** is a supporter of his, while **to blairize** is to do something in the manner of the PM, or to approach things from a New Labour perspective.

■ Martha Stewart

American author, magazine publisher, and house-and-home guru, Martha Stewart has become quite literally a household name. As a noun, a **Martha Stewart** is someone who is extremely enthusiastic and capable, while the verb **to Martha Stewart** (most often used as **Martha Stewarting**) means to tidy up or make wholesome.

> *He's like the Martha Stewart of personal finance, a great doer and a great explainer.* — *Vanity Fair*, 1999.

■ Isabella Blow

Blow is the flamboyant style guru famous for her collection of hats. Overheard at London Fashion Week in 2003 was the simple phrase **to be blowed**, describing the fate of sitting behind someone with a large hat at a show.

■ Mike Tyson

The American heavyweight boxer is remembered in language more for his fighting prowess than for any other more controversial areas of his life. **The Mike Tyson** of a field is its strongest participant.

> *Prof Hugh Pennington, of the medical microbiology department at Aberdeen University, described the disease as the 'Mike Tyson' of viruses, which was 'pretty good' at spreading itself.*
> — *Daily Telegraph*, 2002.

■ Monica Lewinsky

The former White House intern, who infamously (and according to US law) did not have sexual relations with Bill Clinton, became an almost immediate force in phrase and idiom at the time of the impeachment trial. The turn of phrase which seems to have survived is to **Monicaize**, which is to take advantage of someone sexually. More explicitly, to **do a Lewinsky** is to perform fellatio.

■ **John Travolta**

The american actor remains best known for his role in the film *Saturday Night Fever*, in which he played the supreme disco dancer Tony Manero. **A John Travolta** is a master of the dance floor, but the contexts in which his name is used are wide-ranging.

> *It should be the John Travolta of resumes – gyrating its way across the employer's desk, leaving the rest behind like a stack of graceless wallflowers – hspeople.com, 2002.*

■ **Marilyn Monroe**

Unsurprisingly, to be a **Marilyn Monroe** is to be someone extremely sexy and flirtatious. Even a thing can, it seems, be a **Marilyn Monroe**, as in the quotation below.

> *Oestrogen is the Marilyn Monroe of sex hormones … it makes you feel … flirtatious and extremely receptive to sex.*
> – *Cosmopolitan Magazine*, 1998

■ **Delia Smith**

The English cookery expert excited much media attention in 2002 when the use of her name was recognized in a new edition of the *Collins English Dictionary*, whose editors included the idiom **to do a Delia**: to create a meal or recipe inspired by her. The **Delia effect**, the instant surge in sales of an item mentioned on her cookery programme, is also a well known phenomenon in marketing circles.

> *A countrywide boom in sales of skewers, prunes and sweetened condensed milk has been attributed to celebrity chef Delia Smith. According to UK supermarket group Asda, the 'Delia effect' can prove to be a lucrative one for retailers. – Just-Food.com, 2002.*

■ **Agent Dana Scully**

Scully was the sceptical female protagonist of the TV series *The X-Files*, played by Gillian Anderson. The tagline of the series – 'The Truth is Out There' – has passed into the language as a catchphrase, whilst the verb **to Scully** has come to mean to express scepticism about paranormal activity and to look for a scientific rationale.

> *I cannot believe that you of all people are trying to Scully me.*
> – *Buffy the Vampire Slayer*.

■ Gianni Versace

The name of the late Italian fashion designer is still synonymous with innovative and often risqué designs. **To Versace up** is to dress up in glamorous and cutting-edge fashion.

> *She was only taken seriously in male-dominated Hollywood once blanded out, Versace'd up and slimmed down* – Cosmopolitan *Magazine*, 2002.

■ Quentin Tarantino

The director of highly successful films including *Pulp Fiction* and *Reservoir Dogs* has been both criticized and applauded for his emphasis on violence and killing. These characteristics have given rise to the adjective **Quentin Tarantino**, used to describe a mood or sense of danger.

> *'If I had a corpse for every time you've said that....' Despite my bravado it was getting a little Quentin Tarantino around here. 'Now get out of my house,' I bluffed. I opened the garage door. Light flooded in. Rotterman's sleek limousine was slowly sharking up and down the street.* – Kathy Lette, *Alter Ego*, 1998

■ Oprah Winfrey

Such has been the success of the prolific US chat-show host and actress that she has readily stamped her presence on our language. **Oprahization** is the process of making something accessible and instantly available, while **the Oprah effect** is the instant success of a book following recommendation on her televised Book Club (**Oprah-lit**).

> *He inherits a media world far different from the one his father left behind eight years ago, before the explosion of 24-hour news and the Oprahization of politics.* – New York Times, 2001

■ Adlai Stevenson

Stevenson was the veteran American politician and diplomat who tried to convince the Security Council in 1962 that the Soviet Union had positioned nuclear missiles over Cuba. Using black and white aerial pictures, his speech became a historic standard for diplomatic coups. The phrase **an Adlai Stevenson moment**, meaning the definitive evidence of wrongdoing, was used in the coverage of the build-up to the Second Gulf War, and was said to be lacking in Colin Powell's presentation of the rationale for war on Iraq.

■ Charlie Dimmock

A British presenter on a highly successful gardening series, Dimmock enjoys huge popularity in the UK as a result of her down-to-earth (and bra-less) approach. To be **the Charlie Dimmock** of a subject is to be its popular face.

> *Art, along with gardening and D.I.Y., is apparently the new rock n' roll, so does that make Tracey Emin the Charlie Dimmock of the art world?* – Britart.com.

■ Damien Hirst

The name of the controversial British artist, best known for his experimental works involving animal parts, has become shorthand for someone who successfully pushes their art to the limits.

> *Described as 'The Damien Hirst' of ballet, Matthew Bourne is taking the dance scene by storm – rewriting dance conventions and pulling in the crowds to boot.* – BBCi, 2003.

■ Nigella Lawson

Known as 'the domestic goddess', Nigella is the British equivalent of Martha Stewart, but with an added dimension of sexiness and glamour. A **Nigella** of a field is a glamorous master of that trade.

> *She wants her publicity images, featuring a pouting Gorr in black lace with a messy handful of mashed cherries, to make her the Nigella Lawson of cabaret.* – smh.com.au, 2003, on singer Libi Gorr.

17.

Dinky Dirts and Tony Blairs: Rhyming Slang in the 2000s

RHYMING SLANG IS alive and well. Old and much-loved chestnuts are enjoying a new lease of life, and the impulse to create new ones is arguably more powerful than ever. New translations are even being made, and into rather than out of rhyming slang. Mike Coles, an East London religious education teacher, sought to keep the message of the Bible alive by producing in 2000 a rhyming slang version of St Mark's Gospel: 'Jesus took the Uncle Fred (bread) and the Lillian Gish (fish) and fed it to the 5,000'. His project prompted a rare level of secular interest in matters of Christian publishing and is proof of the pulling power that rhyming slang still possesses.

Cockney rhyming slang, which some believe began as a secret language in the criminal underworld of the 16th, 17th, and 18th centuries, had by the end of the 19th century become firmly associated with the language of London street-traders. It remained there as a micro-language for some time, and enjoyed little public profile until the greater mobility of the British population in the late 1900s took it further afield. By the beginning of the 20th century it was centre-stage, both for its colour and for its inherent comedy.

Rhyming slang is the result of conscious word-play rather than the organic evolution evident in other forms of language. John Ayto, in his informative and greatly entertaining *Dictionary of Rhyming Slang* (OUP, 2002), calls the process 'part of a giant ongoing word-game'. Whilst much of the rhyming slang used today carries invisible quotation marks – we do not use, for example, 'apples and pears' without silent acknowledgement to old Cockney – English still reflects an enthusiasm for new coinages. The strongest trend in the 2000s is to create rhymes on the names of a celebrity, whether a pop star – 'popney rhyming slang' – or anyone who has attracted fame or notoriety. The attributes of the celebrity in question are often irrelevant: it is their name that counts, although the most amusing and successful rhymes do make a connection with their subject. The rhymes are also usually straightforward – 'Ruby Murray' for 'curry', for example – but there are examples too of successful rhymes which you need to work a little harder at to decipher, such as a 'Pavarotti' for a ten pound note or 'tenner' (tenor). This has long been one of the attractions of rhyming slang: its meaning is not always obvious, but rather than being a hostile code designed to exclude others, it simply encourages a little mental arithmetic in its translation.

Newspapers such as 'The Currant Bun' (*The Sun*), and TV and film output such as *Only Fools and Horses* and *Lock, Stock and Two Smoking Barrels*, have done much to popularize modern slang and popney in particular. In recent times the tongue-in-cheek term 'Mockney' has emerged, describing a person who affects a cockney accent. Jamie Oliver, Guy Ritchie, and Tony Blair have all been called 'Mockneys'.

Rhyming slang is, however, no longer exclusive to Britain. Australia took to developing new slang with particular enthusiasm at the end of the 19th century, and remains a vibrant source of new vocabulary today. 'Mud and ooze' (booze), 'Cobar shower' (flower), and 'Barry Crocker' (shocker) are a few recent Australian creations, coloured by local preoccupations and allusions. In the US, rhyming slang is less well-known and not the subject of new development, but it does remain part of the traditional image of the 'Cor-Blimey' Briton.

RHYMING PERSONALITIES

Mae West	breast
Betty Grable	table
Fred Astaire	chair
Tony Blairs	flares
Doris Day	gay
Basil Fawlty	balti
Gregory Peck	cheque
Boutros-Boutros Ghali	charlie (cocaine)
Steffi Graf	laugh
Raquel Welch	belch
Clare Rayners	trainers
Jeremy Beadle	to needle
Darren Gough	cough
Damon Hill	pill
Seamus Heaney	bikini
Wyatt Earp	burp
Russell Crowe	go ('to have a Russell Crowe at someone')
Jack Dee	pee
Al Pacino	cappuccino
Ruby Murray	curry
Brad Pitt	shit
Camilla Parker Bowles	Rolls (Royce)
Calvin Klein	wine
Jerry Springer	minger (an ugly person)
Shania Twain	pain ('what a Shania Twain in the backside')
Billy Ocean	suntan lotion
Pete Tong	wrong ('it's all gone a bit Pete Tong')
Britney Spears	beers
Becks and Posh	nosh

18.

Free Comment: The Art of the Headline

Norman Mailer famously said that 'once a newspaper touches a story, the facts are lost forever, even to the protagonists'. That statement, together with the Labour politician Aneurin Bevan's line 'I read the newspapers avidly. It is my one form of continuous fiction', suggests that a checklist of memorable newspaper headlines would not give an entirely accurate view of our recent history. If detailed accuracy is not always the primary consideration of headline writers, we can still admire their linguistic skills – tabloids such as *The Sun* in the UK and the *National Enquirer* in the US have raised snappy headline writing to an art form.

Recent headlines suggest an even more explicit alliance with art in their conscious play on evocative film titles. The story which became known as 'Cheriegate', based on Cherie Blair's dealings with the convicted fraudster Peter Foster over a property deal, prompted the headline 'The Conman, his Lover, and the Prime Minister's Wife', a clever take on Peter Greenaway's film *The Cook, the Thief, His Wife & Her Lover*. 'Privates on Parade' was another direct reference to cinematic fiction, this time in a headline run by the Guardian to describe the sense of unreal glamour created by media coverage of the Gulf War. This blurring of the line between fiction and reality makes Bevan's quip seem all the more appropriate today.

Newspaper headlines clearly serve as a record of landmark moments in history, and they can often echo others from the past. One of the most famous US newspaper headlines of all time was the premature announcement of the winner of the 1948 US Presidential election, called wrongly by the *Chicago Tribune* as 'Dewey defeats Truman'. How similar to the painfully prolonged election of 2000, when the *Miami Herald* ran the headline 'Bush wins it', only to have to change the final edition to 'It's Not Over Yet'. And *The Sun*'s headline 'Got him!', on the toppling of Saddam Hussein's regime, carried deliberate echoes of their cry of victory for the Falklands, 'Gotcha!', twenty years before.

In current times, there is a clear move by the traditionally more sober broadsheets towards the punning headlines previously the preserve of the tabloids. The lines 'Between a Bok and a hard place', referring to the predicament of the Welsh rugby team against the South Africans, and 'Officials say atoll will do nicely', on the fraudulent sale of some small Pacific islands, are both examples from this century from the pages of the serious-thinking *Guardian*. Alliteration has become another important device in headline-writing: 'Flying Fatties Forced To Pay At Last', on the introduction of a rule that obese people pay for two seats on aeroplanes, is a case in point.

Below are some of the best examples of the headline writer's art, both from this century and the last. Inevitably, those of recent times, like so much else in current language, are dominated by the theme of war.

21st-century headlines

Named, Shamed
News of the World on 23 July 2000, announcing a campaign to publish the names and addresses of alleged convicted paedophiles.

America Attacked
Newsday, 11 September 2001, on the terrorist attacks on the World Trade Center and the Pentagon.

This party isn't just dead ... it is totally plucked
The Sun, 18 December 2002, about the apparent disarray in Britain's Tory Party.

Sex, drugs, violence ... and that's just the TV presenters
Leader in *The Sun*, 26 October 2002, a week when a number of TV
stars were shamed for their extra-curricular activities.

15,000 ... by first post. Are you listening now, Mr Blair?
Daily Mirror, 23 January 2003, as part of their campaign against war
in Iraq.

Axis of Weasels
New York Post, 24 January 2003, alongside manipulated images
showing French and German diplomats with weasel heads.

Oh what a lovely war!
Daily Mirror, 27 March 2003, in criticism of the 'smirking, cross-eyed
fool in the White House'.

Toppled!
Daily Mirror, 9 April 2003, on the bringing down of a statue of
Saddam Hussein following the successful occupation of Baghdad by
US troops.

Saving Private Jessica
Time magazine (and others), April 6 2003, on the rescue of Private
Jessica Lynch from her Iraqi captors.

Dances with Wolfowitz
Leader in the *NY Times*, 9 April 2003, commenting on the zeal of
Deputy Secretary of Defense Paul Wolfowitz, and other Bush
administration 'hawks', for more action following success in Iraq.

Jailed? We don't want to give you that!
Sun headline 8 April 2003, after three people accused of cheating on
the TV quiz 'Who Wants to be a Millionaire?' were each given a
suspended sentence.

God save Tony Blair
Editorial, *New York Daily News*, 9 March 2003

Sars Wars
Sun headline on the discovery of the first case of SARS (severe acute respiratory syndrome) in Britain.

Say It Ain't So-Sa!
Chicago Sun Times, 4 June 2003, after baseball player Sammy Sosa was ejected from a game for using a corked bat. The headline echoes a famous headline from 1919: 'Say it ain't so, Joe,' used when Shoeless Joe Jackson was accused of cheating.

We want shirt off your Beck
Sun headline, 13 June 2003, on an apparent offer from A C Milan to sign up the celebrated English footballer David Beckham.

Sex It Up!
Daily Mirror, 30 May 2003, the day after the British government was accused of embellishing intelligence reports on Iraq.

From the last century

Wall Street lays an egg
Variety on 30 October 1929, on the Wall Street crash.

It's that man again…! At the head of a calvacade of seven black motor cars Hitler swept out of his Berlin Chancellery last night on a mystery journey
Headline in the *Daily Express*, 2 May 1929. The acronym ITMA became the title of a BBC radio show.

King's Moll Reno'd in Wolsey's Home Town
US newspaper on Wallis Simpson's divorce proceedings in Ipswich in 1936.

Whose finger do you want on the trigger?
Daily Mirror on 21 September 1951, referring to the atom bomb.

Egghead weds hourglass
Headline in *Variety* 1956, attributed, on the marriage of Arthur Miller and Marilyn Monroe.

It is a moral issue
Times leader on 11 June 1963, commenting on the resignation of the British politician John Profumo following revelations of his affair with society 'mistress' Christine Keeler.

Who breaks a butterfly on a wheel?
Times leader 1 June 1967, defending Mick Jagger after his arrest for cannabis possession, and quoting from Alexander Pope.

The filth and the fury
Daily Mirror, 2 November 1976, following a notorious interview with The Sex Pistols live on Thames Television, echoing William Faulkner's novel *The Sound and the Fury* (itself an allusion to Shakespeare's *Macbeth*).

GOTCHA!
The Sun, 4 May 1982, on the sinking of the *General Belgrano* during the Falklands conflict.

Freddie Starr ate my hamster
Headline in *The Sun*, 13 March 1986.

Starr Wars
Many online and print newspapers ran this headline in the late 1980s to describe former prosecutor Kenneth Starr's alleged witchhunt against Bill Clinton.

If Kinnock wins today will the last person to leave Britain please turn out the lights
The Sun, on election day 9 April 1992, showing the Labour Party leader Neil Kinnock's head inside a lightbulb.

Killer bug ate my face
Daily Star in 1994, on the apparent impending epidemic in the UK of a deadly, flesh-eating superbug.

It's the Sun Wot Won It
The Sun, following the Conservative Party's victory in the 1992 general election.

19.

Sticks and Stones

❝ A nickname is the heaviest stone the Devil can throw at a man. ❞

William Hazlitt (1778-1830), English essayist

NICKNAMES ARE STRONG indicators of the preoccupations of their time. Whether playful or serious, they articulate an immediate response to something culturally significant or amusing. Those that work sum up the aspect of an individual which has captured public attention, and eventually become a kind of shorthand for the person themselves. *Bloody Mary* (Mary Tudor) is a nickname as evocative of the period she lived in as of the individual herself.

Hazlitt makes no bones about the unpleasantness the ownership of an unkind nickname can bring, and some – such as *Attila the Hen* for Margaret Thatcher – can be particularly effective in reinforcing negative associations. *Wacko Jacko* (Michael Jackson), *Slick Willy* (Bill Clinton), and *Hanoi Jane* (Jane Fonda) might also belong in that category. Many, however, are coined with affection, and are worn by their recipients with pride long after the prowess or event which prompted them has vanished. Indeed a nickname can be of high commercial value, and usurpers of the title need to be fought off. If Madonna is said to hate her nickname *Madge*, others are highly defensive of their moniker, as seen in the case of **Posh v Posh** in 2003, when a bid to register the phrase as a trademark by the East Anglian football club Peterborough United (referred to by its fans as

'The Posh' since it was established 68 years before) was contested by former Spice Girl Victoria 'Posh' Beckham, who claimed the nickname as hers.

The greatest coiners of nicknames today are the tabloids, whose bid to label celebrities for the sake of punchy headlines has resulted in some of the most imaginative epithets of recent times. Some labels are so successful that they spawn copy-cat nicknames: *Two Brains*, the epithet given to the intellectual and policy-maker David Willetts, found strong echoes in the rather more unfortunate *Two Jags* label given to Deputy Prime Minister John Prescott while he was Environment Minister and owner of two government cars (prompting the then opposition leader William Hague to remark that Prescott's 'idea of a park and ride scheme is to park one Jaguar and ride another'). The next link in the chain was the media's dubbing of Prescott as *Two Jabs*, following his punching of an egg-throwing protester. Finally, at least for now, the sequence continued when the questionable property deal in the 'Cheriegate' affair, in which Cherie Blair unwittingly enlisted the help of a convicted conman to purchase a flat for her son, prompted the line: 'Tut, tut, two flats Tony' from *The Guardian* newspaper.

In the US, baseball is home to some of the most colourful sporting nicknames of our time. Some of the best examples include *Say Hey Kid* (Willie Mays), *The Thrill* (Will Clark), *The Straw that Stirs the Drink* (Reggie Jackson), *Slammin'* (Sammy Sosa), *The Big Hurt* (Frank Thomas), *The Bash Brothers* (Mark McGwire and Jose Canseco), and *Louisiana Lightning* (Ron Guidry).

The following list of nicknames includes some of those which have already proved themselves, together with some contemporary monikers which may not prove so enduring, for all their entertainment value now.

Bambi: Tony Blair, whose youth and relative inexperience when first elected leader of the Labour Party led to this epithet, coined after the young deer in Felix Salten's story for children and the Disney film of the same name. The nickname did not prove long-lasting, with Blair being criticized for his authoritarian style of leadership, prompting him to say of himself at a party conference: 'Hard for me, sometimes: 1994, Bambi; 1995, Stalin. From Disneyland to dictatorship in 12 short months. I'm not sure which one I prefer.'

Dubya: George Walker Bush. To distinguish himself from his father and former US President, the son is widely known as George W. Bush or simply George W. 'Dubya' is the imitation of the pronunciation of the letter 'W' in Bush's home state of Texas. US columnist Molly Ivins has given Bush a further nickname: **Shrub**, a reflection of her view that he is the smallest (intellectually and politically) of the Bush family.

The Prince of Darkness: Peter Mandelson, British Labour politician and the acknowledged master of spin-doctoring. For this reason he also became known as *The Sultan of Spin*. The nickname *Prince of Darkness* has also been applied in recent times to the US foreign policy adviser Richard Perle, who resigned as Chairman of the Pentagon's influential Defence Policy Board following revelations of his business links to a firm which stood to profit from the war in Iraq.

The Body: Elle McPherson, the Australian model with an enviable physique.

The Iron Chancellor: British Chancellor of the Exchequer Gordon Brown. His nickname was almost self-coined: he promised while still in opposition to have an 'iron commitment to macroeconomic stability and financial prudence' should Labour come to power. The use of the title *Iron Chancellor* is in deliberate imitation of that given to Otto von Bismarck, the Chancellor of Germany and the driving force of its unification in the 19th century.

Dr Death: Harold Frederick Shipman, the British serial killer judged in 2000 to be responsible for the deaths of at least 215 patients over a 23 year period. This name was given to him by the British tabloids during his trial. In the US, euthanasia advocate and practitioner Jack Kevorkian is also known as *Dr Death*.

Goldenballs: David Beckham, celebrated English footballer and one half of the media couple 'Posh and Becks'. This nickname was apparently a private one given to him by his wife Victoria Beckham, until she revealed all in an interview with chat-show host Michael Parkinson, when it became the hot property of the tabloids.

Hollywood: Shane Warne, Australian cricketer and legendary spinner. The nickname suited both his superstar image and the level of press coverage he attracted.

The Cat: English cricketer Phil Tufnell, voted the 'King of the Jungle' in 2003 in the reality TV show *I'm a Celebrity, Get Me Out of Here*. He was given his nickname by his team-mates because of his fondness for naps in the dressing room.

PAPER CUT-OUTS: NICKNAMES FROM THE GULF WAR

The Western media were quick to produce a whole series of nicknames for their 'anti-heroes', following on from the already established label **The Butcher of Baghdad** for Saddam Hussein. One of the most-used epithets was **Comical Ali** for Iraq's former information minister Mohammed Saeed al-Sahaf, who became a media star during the war thanks to his unwavering optimism and his vivid use of language. This nickname is a play on the more sinister one of **Chemical Ali**, given to General Ali Hassan al-Majid for his role in attacks on Kurds in northern Iraq in 1988. That also promoted the association in the name **Chemical Sally**, given to Professor Huda Salih Mahdi Ammash, Iraq's top biological weapons expert.

Finally, BBC correspondent Rageh Omar became a cult figure during the conflict due to his 'irresistible combination of good looks and bravery' (*Daily Mirror*). The nickname given to the subject of 'Ragehmania' was simply **The Scud Stud**.

Some of the best nicknames from the past

The Flying Peacemaker: Henry Kissinger, statesman and Democrat, known for his style of 'shuttle diplomacy', whereby he flew between nations in conflict in order to mediate, as he did during his successful negotiations for the withdrawal of US troops from South Vietnam.

The Juice: O. J. Simpson, former US American football player and considered to be one of the greatest running backs of all time. 'Juice' derived both from his name and from his ability to squeeze out of tight spaces: the latter association proved useful to journalists during Simpson's trial for the murder of his ex-wife Nicole Brown and her boyfriend, a charge from which he was eventually acquitted.

The Comeback Kid: Bill Clinton, 42nd President of the United States. This nickname, one of several, was first used by Clinton himself following his defeat in the Democratic primary in New Hampshire in 1992. The phrase encapsulated his determination to recover from what was a major setback, and proved to be needed during his term as President and further reversals of fortune.

The Bouncing Czech: Robert Maxwell, the Czechoslovakian-born media tycoon who died under mysterious circumstances in 1991, after which it emerged that he had misappropriated the pension funds of many of his newspaper companies.

Gazza: Paul Gascoigne, English footballer. He was an exceptionally gifted midfielder who attracted media attention for his exploits both on and off the pitch. His nickname, coined by the British Press, has showed remarkable staying power.

The Animated Meringue: Dame Barbara Cartland, prolific writer of romantic novels and lover of pink, fluffy clothes and heavy make-up.

The Bronx Bull: Jake LaMotta, US boxer and former world middle-weight champion. His nickname comes from his birthplace and his aggressive technique of making a low-crouching charge in the ring. He is also known as the **Raging Bull**, and was played by Robert De Niro in Martin Scorsese's film of the same name.

Paddy Pantsdown: Paddy Ashdown, former leader of the Liberal Democrats. 'Paddy Pantsdown' was a *Sun* headline on 6 February 1992, following revelations of an affair between Ashdown and his former secretary.

The People's Princess: Diana, Princess of Wales. The name was originally coined by Julie Burchill and was later popularized in a quote from Tony Blair on her death in 1997: 'She was the People's Princess, and that is how she will stay in our hearts and our memories forever.'

The Greatest: Muhammad Ali (born Cassius Clay), US boxer. In his prime Ali was a notorious self-promoter, with 'I am the greatest' becoming his catchphrase. Ali was also known as the **Louisville Lip** (he was born in Louisville, Kentucky and sported a robe stitched with the label **The Lip** in his first heavyweight world title fight), **Gaseous Cassius**, and **The Mouth**.

Mr Dynamite: James Brown, known for his powerful stage presence. He is also known as **The Godfather of Soul** for his role as a musical innovator.

MORE THAN ONE NICKNAME: FAME OR NOTORIETY?

Margaret Thatcher
The Blessed Margaret
Attila the Hen
The Grocer's Daughter
The Iron Lady
The Leaderene
Maggie
The Milk Snatcher (after she cut back on free school milk)
Tina (acronym for 'There is no alternative')

20.

Apostrophe Catastrophes: New Trends in Grammar and Usage

❝ Correct English is the slang of prigs who write history and essays. ❞

George Eliot

ENGLISH IS A DEMOCRATIC language, in which vocabulary and grammar change according to the pressures of usage. Unlike many of its European counterparts, it is not governed by any single body. At a time when other nations were safeguarding their linguistic heritage by forming national 'academies', the most influential users of English spoke out against a similar institution for their mother tongue. 'A keeper of English', wrote the English grammarian and theologian Joseph Priestley, 'would be unsuitable to the genius of a free nation'.

By 'correct' English today, we usually mean standard English, the form of the language that is used in government, education, and other formal contexts. In fact, given that there is no enforcer of grammar and vocabulary, standard English is simply one form of English sitting alongside other, less formal, varieties. It is not prescribed, nor are its rules constant over time: constructions slip in and out of favour throughout history, so that whilst the British 'ain't' might now be associated with uneducated speech, it was once a word of royalty, used by the kings and queens of Britain. Equally, until the 18th century it was correct (and logical) to say 'you was' when referring to one person.

A lack of a single authority does not, however, diminish our desire for some ground rules and for some yardstick against which to measure blatant contraventions of standard style and usage. If the argument over the split infinitive has lost relevance in current times, there are still many bones of contention to take its place. The misuse of apostrophes, the decline of the semicolon, and the likely extinction of the subjunctive are all bêtes noires of grammatical purists. Film and media star Liz Hurley's infamous quote 'If I were as fat as Marilyn Monroe I should kill myself' was for some notable more for its hyper-correct use of the subjunctive ('I should' rather than the more usual 'I would') than for its controversial view on body weight. Perhaps the real issue is not so much that grammatical correctness is outdated, but rather that the drivers of usage have changed: the priority is now clear communication and the avoidance of ambiguity rather than an adherence to rules set out by grammarians.

Whilst the spotlight will almost always fall upon new words, grammar and syntax are equally likely to change. The following represent some of the most notable recent evolutions within our language. Some may turn out to be syntactical novelties, whilst others are likely to show some permanence.

Apostrophes

The misuse of the apostrophe is a cause of great irritation to some. There are numerous websites, such as that created by the 'Apostrophe Protection Society', which devote themselves exclusively to exposing apostrophe abuse. As with hyphens, apostrophes are being used in different ways rather than becoming lost altogether, although there are some signs of their fading from view, at least in their hitherto 'correct' forms.

People are often confused as to when to use an apostrophe, and the result of the confusion can be overuse rather than underuse. So *MOT's while you wait!*, *Delicious Pizza's to Take Away*, and *The deal will significantly enhance it's position in the market*, are all part of recent evidence of over-enthusiasm (*MOTs*, *Pizzas*, and *its* would have been correct).

Essentially an apostrophe has two functions: to indicate possession (*the boy's ball*), and as a contraction of two words

(*I'm* for *I am*, *aren't* for *are not*, etc.). Possessive *adjectives* – *yours*, *hers*, *his*, *its*, and *theirs* – do not require apostrophes. These established standards for apostrophes are often undermined by large corporations who play around with language in order to best achieve their commercial aims. The apostrophe is often omitted in company names (e.g. Barclays Bank), a trend perhaps started by designers in the 1980s when the apostrophe was simply too much clutter. Microsoft was once blamed for the growing misuse of apostrophes in plural acronyms (such as AIDS) because their spell-checking software automatically converted the form into a possessive (AID's).

Quotation marks

One characteristic of modern prose in informal contexts is an abundant use of quotation marks, used for emphasis rather than for the reporting of any speech. The effect can be to cast doubt over the word between the quotation marks – the opposite in fact of the endorsement the user is looking for. *Please 'Do Not' Deposit Cash*, and *Containing 'real' bacon bits* are good examples.

'Think Different'

One of the most common transgressions of standard English is the use of an adjective where an adverb should be. The greatest offenders are often advertisers who regard an adverb as adding unnecessary length and lacking in bite, as evidenced in the above 1998 slogan for Apple Computers. Sports commentary often offers up good examples too: *he's done excellent* is common praise in football banter.

Hyphens

The changing preferences for hyphenation provide an interesting example of language on the move and of the continuum in shifts of usage. Whilst the hyphenation of compounds is fast dying out (*carpark*, *newsreader*, and *punchline* were all previously hyphenated), new hyphens are being introduced in surprising places. This last phenomenon is most striking in phrasal verbs: verbs which are combined with a preposition or adverb and which have different meanings as a result. A growing – and incorrect – trend in English today is to include hyphens in verb uses, as in *we need to set-up a new meeting*, or *the advice is to continue to build-up your pension*.

Until recently any modifying use of a noun (where it precedes and modifies the meaning of another noun) was signalled with a hyphen – *fish-shop*, for example, not *fish shop*. Even street signs were once predominantly hyphenated – *Canal-Street, Jermyn-Street*. Today, nouns are not only used attributively without hyphens (*action movie*, for example), but they are also often piled high one upon the other without any punctuation at all. Newspapers are a rich source of examples of the trend – *missing person death shock horror evidence probe* would be a model – and not too far-fetched – example.

Punctuation

Two areas of punctuation most likely to confuse and be confused are the **colon** and **semicolon**. The movement away from the colon began in informal contexts when a dash became the preferred equivalent of what is essentially an 'equals' sign. This trend is now firmly established in more formal writing too, and the colon may well be on the path to extinction.

He could not have explained his optimism – he was happy and therefore bound to succeed. – Ian McEwan, *Atonement*, 2001

The semicolon, used to separate statements too distinct for a comma but too closely related for a period or full stop (or syntactically to separate two complex clauses), is also falling out of favour. Today's prose is influenced by the demands of the soundbite and of plain English, both of which argue against richly textured sentences punctuated by semicolons.

Commas are used haphazardly in much of today's language. Even professional writers are adopting an idiosyncratic approach: some will use a lot of commas, while others very few. An emerging trend is the use of an opening bracketing comma, and the omission of the second, when referring to the subject of a sentence. So *the Newcastle manager, Bobby Robson, said* is fine, but *the Newcastle manager, Bobby Robson said* is not.

'Fillers'

A 'filler' is a linguistic structure that fills a particular slot in dialogue or prose and which contributes more to rhythm than to meaning. Fillers function as a kind of check with the person one is talking to, but then become an individualistic form of expression and indeed one of the mannerisms that satirists pick up in a public person (*y'know*, for example, has become a noted part of Tony Blair's speech).

One of the best examples of a filler in everyday and increasing use is *innit?*. The word arose as an informal way of saying *isn't it?*, but more recently it has developed into a general-purpose – and some would say ungrammatical – filler used to seek confirmation of a statement or for emphasis, as in *you'd better hurry on over, innit?* (meaning *hadn't you?*). The latest development on this line is an interrogative *is it?* on the part of the other speaker. So *'I went to that club'* is met with *'Is it?'* instead of *'Did you?'*.

Another current favourite, which has been around for over a decade but which has recently been taken up with great enthusiasm, is the word *like*, as in *She was like 'Don't look at me', and he was like 'What!'*. It is particularly characteristic of 'Valspeak', the language of the so-called 'Valley girls' of America which emerged in the 1980s and which was parodied to great effect in such films as *Clueless* (1995). The following lyrics from Frank and Moon Zappa's 1982 song *Valley Girl* is a good example of 'Valspeak' taken to its extreme.

> Like, OH MY GOD! (Valley Girl)
>
> Like – TOTALLY (Valley Girl)
>
> Encino is like SO BITCHEN (Valley Girl)
>
> There's like the Galleria (Valley Girl)
>
> And like all these like really great shoe stores
>
> I love going into like clothing stores and stuff
>
> I like buy the neatest mini-skirts and stuff
>
> It's like so BITCHEN cuz like everybody's like
>
> Super-super nice
>
> It's like so BITCHEN

Tense swapping

An emerging pattern in current speech is to replace the present tense with the continuous present, and in particular with verbs of approval such as to *like* and to *love*. A trend which has existed for a while has been the almost self-parodic use of the continuous present tense in such phrases as: *I am so not loving that*. However, the swapping of tenses is now becoming a more serious phenomenon, and *I'm liking that* is a turn of phrase which is establishing itself in all sorts of contexts – from offices to weblogs – without apparent irony.

Intensifiers

These words are used so frequently that they begin to behave rather like fillers, but they fulfil a different function by reinforcing the adjective that follows them. *So*, *totally*, *well*, and *literally* are all recent examples of intensifiers.

The boy looked in wonder at the polyurethane and leather marvel and offered it the coolest of street compliments. 'Well wicked', he breathed. – Daily Telegraph, 1990.

Chat-room grammar

Email, and especially chat room, communication is often ungrammatical due to its informality. It is highly personalized and conversational in nature, and sentences often follow patterns typical of speech, with features including full stops in non-standard places (e.g. *S'never gonna pass it's* [sic] *MOT next month. Not without a new pump*) and the disregard of sentence breaks and full stops. Messages tend to reflect the sender's thought processes as they compose the message, as in *I know nothing a web site is prolly better save asking different stuff here every 2 seconds*.

In addition, informality or light-heartedness is signalled by the user's choice of spelling – correct forms often being less favoured than phonetic or semi-phonetic spellings (*the shop seems to have bin closed for a cuppla daze innit*). Other features of spelling and punctuation include the writing of two or more words as one (*abit, alittle, alot*) and the omission of the apostrophe (*dont* instead of *don't*, *isnt* rather than *isn't*, etc.).

Time will tell whether these departures from standard grammar will begin to intrude upon more formal writing.

Journalistic licence

Newspaper headline-writers have always prioritized impact over grammatical correctness, whilst news bulletins on radio and television have traditionally stayed loyal to the standards of 'proper' English, or BBC English as it is known in the UK. The situation would appear to be changing, however, for there now appears to be a growing tendency amongst newsreaders – particularly in the US – to omit the verb 'to be' in their oral headlines. Michael Kinsley, in his article 'Is Disappearing: What TV news doing to our precious verbs', cites some introductory soundbites given by Lou Dobbs at the top of one of his CNN shows in 2002 as cases in point, including *Top government officials today adding their voices to the call for Americans to remain vigilant!* He notes that this trend joins those already established conventions of 'journalese' which include the use of historic present (*House Passes Tax Cut*), and the transposition of time element and verb (*The Governor Thursday announced he would resign*).

The above represents only a selection of changes in linguistic behaviour. In the middle of the last century, the nearest equivalent of language authorities for the English language were lamenting over the use of such words as *racial, television,* and *commentate.* Perhaps the only thing we can predict with any certainty today is that the next hundred years will undoubtedly produce their own controversies.

21.

Crossing Continents: US English

❝ The English and the American language and literature are both good things; but they are better apart than mixed. ❞

H W and F G Fowler, *The King's English*, 1931

BILL BRYSON, IN HIS study *Mother Tongue*, estimates that some 4,000 everyday words are used differently between the US and the UK. Whilst this may seem a very large number, it is worth remembering that there was a point early in the 20th century, before the unprecedented impact of modern communication, when some language authorities were expecting American English to evolve into an entirely separate language altogether. Clearly this did not materialize, and whilst it is said that some isolated pockets of America – communities in the Appalachian hills for example – retain the vocabulary and speech patterns of Elizabethan England, the influences of both Englishes upon each other is a continuously evolving process.

The availability of 24/7 news, and the global reach of the Internet, have brought about dramatic changes in the way words travel. When conducting its fieldwork in the 1960s, the *Dictionary of American Regional English* – an enormous undertaking to record the dialects of the American people – searched for individuals who had been brought up in one particular region by parents who had experienced the same. It would be an almost impossible task to find that purity of linguistic environment today, and to find people who have escaped exposure to wide varieties of American English through television and other modern media.

The British have historically been hostile to the adoption of American words. American English was the first body of non-British English to become a dominant worldwide linguistic force, and so to be seen as a challenger – if not adulterator – of British English. Yet the influence of American usage and American spelling has been profound, and by far the majority of words introduced into English over the past two hundred years have travelled from west to east. Film, television, and music are among the primary media for new American vocabulary, through which the assimilation of new words is often an unconscious but highly effective process.

American English itself is made up of many varieties. Given an area of more than three million square miles populated by over two hundred million people, it is unsurprising that the spoken language varies enormously. There is a norm which might be termed standard American English, but there are also many other internal influences at work including Yiddish, American Jewish English, and Black English or 'Ebonics'. The subject of much debate as to its definition – is it a language in its own right, or a dialect? – Black English has had a particularly strong influence on British English and on other languages. It is associated with prominent areas of culture: as the language of jazz and blues in early times, and now of hip-hop and rap. While it shares most of its grammar and vocabulary with other dialects of English, it is distinct in many ways, and it is arguably more different from standard English than any other dialect spoken in continental North America.

This section offers a snapshot of those words which have gained momentum in the US in recent years. Many of them are likely to cross the Atlantic and to gain currency in British English; in time the point of origin will become blurred and ultimately irrelevant. The trends in new-word coining are, unsurprisingly, not dissimilar to those in Britain, although there are differing degrees of emphasis depending on the different cultural influences at work. Formation areas include wireless and telecom, new ways of working and childcare, and our relationship to food and health. Some words belong to earlier times but have found new resonance (e.g. *POTUS*), whilst some of the most striking new terms are extensions of existing expressions: *stained glass ceiling*, *blue dog Democrat*, *bridezilla* and *smoke-easy*.

blue dog Democrat: a Democrat in the US from a Southern state and who has a conservative voting record. The term derives from the name of a coalition of Southern Democrats in the US Congress formed in 1995, and alludes to an older term, *yellow dog Democrat*, for a party loyalist who allegedly 'would vote for a yellow dog if it were on the ballot as a Democrat.' The *blue dog Democrats* claim that their conservative views have been choked off by their own party to the point that these yellow dogs have turned blue.

bootylicious: attractive; 'booty' is slang for 'buttocks'.

bridezilla: an overzealous bride-to-be who changes for the worse in the course of wedding preparations. The term is a blend of bride and the name of the monster from the cartoon and film *Godzilla*.

The tricky thing about bridezillas is that their transition from sweethearts to creatures from hell cannot be foreseen, not even by the future husbands. – Dallas Morning News, 2002.

camgirl: a girl or woman who poses for a webcam.

cell yell: loud talking on a cell phone.

Wireless technology has made it easier than ever to learn more about a perfect stranger's life. All you have to do is to walk around in the 21st century in any industrialized nation in the world and listen for 'cell yell'. – Los Angeles Times, 2002.

club sandwich generation: a generation of people responsible for the care of their children, grandchildren, and parents or other ageing relatives. The term is an extension of *sandwich generation*, a generation responsible for the care of their children and parents: a club sandwich uses three pieces of bread.

cube farm: a large open-plan office divided into cubicles for individual workers.

dark biology: scientific research related to biological weapons.

diaper dandy: a person who attains fame or recognition at an extremely young age. The phrase came into recent prominence when the 18-year-old basketball player LeBron James entered the National Basketball Association on leaving high school.

> *The problem is that we corrupted LeBron James … We made him into a star before he even set foot on an NBA court … hailing him as the ultimate diaper dandy.* – Daily Illini, online edition, 2003.

fake bake: the process of getting a sunless tan, such as under sunlamps or by applying a sunless-tanning lotion. The term is also used as a verb, *to fake-bake*.

flannel panel: a section in a magazine, newspaper, or other publication that lists the contributors or advertises the contents.

hardbody: a person with very toned or well-developed muscles.

hysterical realism: realistic fiction that is characterized by overblown prose and intellectual digressions.

> *This is not magical realism. It is hysterical realism. The conventions of realism are not being abolished but, on the contrary, exhausted, and overworked.* – James Wood, The New Republic, 2000, on recent novels.

job spill: a situation in which job-related work or anxiety encroaches on one's leisure time.

killer app: a feature, function, or application of a new technology or product that is presented as virtually indispensable or much superior to rival products.

locarb (of a food or diet): having few or no carbohydrates, especially those from sugar.

losingest (also Canadian): losing more often than others of its kind; least successful.

> *Lenny Wilkens became the National Basketball Association's all-time losingest coach on Friday as the Toronto Raptors fell to the white-hot San Antonio Spurs 124-98.* – espnstar.com, 2003.

mommy track: a career path for women who sacrifice some promotions and pay rises in order to devote more time to raising their children. It contrasts with the idea of 'fast track'.

nanny cam: a webcam or CCTV camera in a private home which allows parents to monitor their childcarer.

orthorexia nervosa: a strict, near-obsessive following of a particular diet or eating regimen.

p-book: a book printed on paper, as distinguished from one in electronic form (*e-book*).

play date: a date and time set by parents for children to play together.

POTUS: President of the United States. This term dates from the early 20th century, but the television series *The West Wing* has done much to bring it back into favour. The corresponding term for the President's wife is *FLOTUS*, the First Lady of the United States.

reasonable woman standard: a guideline for determining what constitutes sexual harassment, based on suppositions about what a reasonable woman would find objectionable.

smoke-easy: a private club, bar, or other place where smokers gather to avoid anti-smoking laws. The word is based on the pattern of *speakeasy*, an illicit drinking club or liquor club during Prohibition.

> *Other smoke-ban municipalities have allowed bars to reorganize as private smoking clubs – 'smoke-easies'. Commissioner Frieden is scornful of such exemptions. 'We don't allow asbestos-easies. We don't allow benzene-easies. We don't allow formaldehyde-easies, or radiation-easies.'* – New York Times, 2002.

stained-glass ceiling: an unofficially acknowledged barrier faced by women who want to enter or be promoted within the clergy. Alternatively the term can mean a discriminatory barrier that prevents a person from advancing in any field because of religious beliefs. The term is a variation of the *glass ceiling*, a barrier to the progression of women in any profession.

tightie-whities: men's white cotton briefs.

22.

Where Global Meets Local: World English

ONE IN FIVE OF THE world's population speaks English with a good level of competence, and the demand from the remaining four-fifths is increasing. English is taking on new forms, just as it has done continuously over the 1,500 years or so of its use. Some see this moment in its history as being particularly critical. Within the next few years the number of people speaking English as a second language will exceed the number of native speakers. This could have a dramatic effect on the evolution of the language: it is those who speak English as an additional language who will determine its future. 'The English Language', writes David Graddol in his excellent and often startling study *The Future of English?* (The British Council, 1997), 'seems set to play an ever more important role in world communications, international business, and social and cultural affairs. But it may not be the native-speaking countries who most benefit.'

In the process of being absorbed by new cultures, English develops to take account of local language needs, giving rise not just to new vocabularies but also to new grammars and pronunciations. These localized Englishes can diverge quite dramatically from the language used in Britain and North America, and the result is a fragmentation and diversity which undermines the traditional view of English as a unifying power. At the same time, there are forces working in the opposite direction, setting global standards for English that make it intelligible to all. One of the most powerful of these is the

Internet, seen by some as the electronic 'flagship' of global English. A recent study has estimated that English is the medium for over 80% of the information stored on the world's computers.

These apparently contradictory trends in the evolution of English, whereby on the one hand global technologies promote a uniform language, and on the other non-native speakers create their own individual pockets of English, are evidence of two of its most important functions. It is a medium of international communication, but it is also a tool which can be adapted to match individual cultural identities. The following examples of words, from some but by no means all of the main 'varieties' of English, demonstrate this latter ability of English to change to fit its environment.

Australasian English

Despite recent distinct divergences in pronunciation, which undermine the notion of a uniform Australasian English, the vocabularies of Australian and New Zealand English are very similar, as are the linguistic influences directing them. Australia in particular is becoming increasingly multi-cultural in its make-up, and the breadth and diversity of its ethnic communities have helped to re-direct the perception of Australian English from the comic stereotyping that is *strine*, a kind of stage Australian with exaggerated vowels and clipped syllables, to something more sophisticated and cosmopolitan. The Australian lexicon has been enriched in the past two decades by words and concepts from indigenous cultures.

Tom McArthur, in his meticulously researched study of World English (*The Oxford Guide to World English*, OUP 2002) shows the line between formal and informal usage in Australasian English as being less sharply drawn than else-where. Such colloquial tendencies as the addition of suffixes such as '-o' and '-ie' – *roughie* (a trick), *plonko* (a drinker of *plonk*), *arvo* (afternoon), *reffo* (refugee) and *barbie* (barbecue) – are freely attached to words even in more formal contexts.

Today's neologisms inevitably highlight the social and

cultural concerns particular to Australasia. Below are a few of those items enjoying currency:

practical reconciliation: the conservative Australian government's term for appropriate reconciliation between indigenous and non-indigenous Australians, focusing on aid programmes that will improve the living standards of indigenous people.

tag dag: a person who mistakenly allows the manufacturer's tag on an item of clothing to be visible. A *dag* is an unfashionable or untrendy person.

Koori Court: (in Victoria) a division of a magistrate's court which allows involvement of the indigenous community in the sentencing of an indigenous person. The term *Koori* became, in the 1960s, the word used by Aboriginals themselves to mean 'Aboriginal people' or 'Aboriginal person': it literally means 'man' in the Aboriginal language Awabakal.

SIEV (acronym): suspected illegal entry vehicle.

> *John Howard categorically assured Australians that SIEV-X sank in Indonesian waters, and proceeded to score heavily against Kim Beazley for daring to suggest that the death by drowning of 353 people could have something to do with us.* – Sydney Morning Herald, 2002.

ute muster: (especially in country towns): a gathering of utility trucks for display and competition. *Ute* is short for utility, and a *muster* is a gathering or meeting. Prizes are awarded in such categories as **best town ute, best chick** (or **sheila's**) **ute** (the best utility truck driven by a woman), and **best feral ute** (a *feral ute* is a dented and bruised utility truck).

budgie smugglers: jocular term for a man's brief and tight-fitting swimming costume.

> *Given that Australians don't have a national dress as such, perhaps we need to adopt budgie-smugglers as our official male costume.* – Rivers Catalogue, 2002.

Canadian English

Canadian society is a plural one which accommodates many different languages, including and beyond the two official languages of French and English, which co-exist with a number of indigenous tongues. Canadian English has its roots in the American English brought to Canada by Loyalists in the American Revolution, and its subsequent evolution is much like that of American English, albeit with somewhat different influences.

Canadian English vocabulary is identified by Tom McArthur as being from three main types: the extension and adaptation of traditional English words put to new uses, adoptions from indigenous languages, and borrowings from French. *Riding*, a term denoting a political constituency and echoing the three *Ridings* of the English county of Yorkshire, *Inuktitut*, the language of the Inuit, and *poutine*, a dish of French fries topped with cheese curd and gravy, exemplify each of these three influences respectively.

Below is a selection of some more recent words and senses emerging in Canadian English.

redirect: a situation in a hospital emergency department whereby ambulances with all but critically ill patients are redirected to another hospital. There have been a number of recent high-profile cases in the past couple of years resulting from understaffing of emergency departments.

> *As of Wednesday afternoon, of the 16 out of 23 hospitals that were turning ambulances away, 10 of those were on critical care bypass. On Tuesday ... seven were on redirect, accepting only critically ill patients.* – The Mirror (North York, Ontario), 2001.

grow op: an illegal marijuana-growing operation, usually in someone's own home.

> *Half the suspects in B.C. grow-ops walk away without any conviction at all, and more than half of those had prior drug convictions. 'The notion that they are mom and pop operations going on in Chilliwack is just not true,' Prof. Plecas says.*
> – Chilliwack Progress, 2002.

Nunavummiut: a person from Nunavut, the area in the arctic region created as a new territory of Canada where the Inuit people would be the majority. The suffix '-iut' means simply 'people of'.

courier parent: a person who obtains a visa to immigrate only so that his or her children may also get immigrant status.

compassion club: a non-profit organization which sells marijuana for medicinal use.

> 'The leader of the federal Marijuana party was busted at the Montreal compassion club for providing medicine to the sick,' says [Party Leader] Mike Patriquen. 'It's an ongoing, constitutional challenge.' — The Packet (Halifax, Nova Scotia), 2001

download: to shift or relegate responsibilities or costs for a programme from one level of government to another. This has been a popular exercise with provincial governments in Canada, which shift the responsibility of delivering certain services to the municipalities in order to give their constituents a tax-cut (and in the hope that an increase in municipal tax to fund the same programme will go un-noticed).

> Alas, not all is idyllic in the city.... The Ontario government is also downloading some services onto the city, although it claims this adjustment will be revenue neutral. — Report in Business Magazine, 1998.

Indian English

It is estimated that India is home to the third-largest English-speaking community in the world. The role of English within a complex multilingual society is far from straightforward: together with Hindi it is used as a 'pan-language' across India, but it can also be a speaker's first, second, or third language, and its features may depend heavily on their ethnicity and caste.

The grammar of Indian English has many distinguishing features, of which perhaps the best-known (and often-parodied) are the use of the present continuous tense, as in 'he is having very much of property', and the use of 'isn't it' as a ubiquitous question tag: 'We are meeting tomorrow, isn't it?' The first example reflects another characteristic of the language, which is to include intrusive articles such as 'in' or 'of' in idiomatic phrases. Verbs are also used differently, with speakers often dropping a preposition or object altogether: 'I insisted immediate payment', while double possessives: 'our these prices' (instead of the British English 'these prices of ours') are commonplace.

The vocabulary of Indian English can be equally resonant of the country's linguistic history.

desh: a person's native land. In Hindi the word means country, while *desi* means 'of or from my country'. Each can be used either as an affectionate term or a mild put-down.

history-sheeter: a person with a criminal record.

Finding himself unable to wait till the preparations for their escape were complete, the 20-year-old history-sheeter ... gave the slip to the policemen who had escorted him to the district and sessions court at Shivajinagar on Saturday afternoon.
— Indian Express, 1999.

mahurat: an auspicious time for an enterprise to begin or for a ceremony to take place. The word is Hindi and originally from the Sanskrit *muhurta*, meaning a division of time (approximately 48 minutes, one thirtieth of a day).

After the land has been selected, the owner should consult a learned astrologer to find out a mahurat to start the construction of the house which would bring him health, wealth, prosperity and good fortune. — thebharat.com, 2003.

prepone: to move something forward in time (the opposite of postpone).

maha: very large or great. From the Sanskrit.

I muttered about how they were going to sell the place to some fucking dairy farmer's son who would give it some maha-groovy name like The Purple Ant Farm. — Vikram Chandra, Love and Longing in Bombay, 1997.

roko: a protest or demonstration.

videshi: made in a country other than India. This Hindi word is often paired with **swadeshi**, meaning made in India from Indian-produced materials, in the saying **all videshi and no swadeshi**.

> *Swadeshi-videshi. The debate rages on and on. Much Coke has flowed under the bridge, and the big Mac has been tamed. Yet ... what is swadeshi and what is videshi? Can anyone really tell the difference?* – Indian Express, 1998.

Caribbean English

Standard British English has traditionally been the linguistic model for the Commonwealth Caribbean, although recently the import of US television, radio, and tourism has made American English an equally powerful influence. Nevertheless, localisms, in the form of the many varieties of Creole, are an equally productive area of Caribbean English. These can take the form of new senses of existing words – so *miserable*, for example, takes on the meaning of *mischievous* – or new coinages altogether. As the Caribbean gains an increasing sense of nationalism, so the Creoles are acquiring new resonance and greater prestige. Below is a very small selection of new words from the local vernacular, many of which have successfully travelled out to Caribbean communities across the world.

criss: smart or fashionable. The word is probably a contraction of crisp.

> *You're gonna look criss in dat dress at de wedding,* – Sis.
> – Alex Wheattle, *East of Acre Lane*, 2001.

facety: rude, arrogant, or excessively bold. The word is probably from the obsolete English word *facey* but has perhaps also been influenced by *feisty*.

nyam: to eat. The word is Jamaican and probably originally referred to the eating of yams (sweet potatoes).

> *When de drink up done, I come fe me biscuits an' the whole lot ah dem nyam!* – Courttia Newland, *Snakeskin*, 2000.

doudou: a term of endearment. The word is French Creole and is an extension of the French word *doux* meaning 'sweet.'

> *Cause, doudou, I didn't had much experience, not much, but I had enough to know sex is the firstest thing they does go for.*
> — Stewart Brown, *The Oxford Book of Short Stories*, 1998.

upful: cheerful and positive.

> *Marley's message was, as he put it, 'upful and bright', but to render 'Talkin Blues' and 'Dem Belly Full', into gleeful work-outs, is to miss the point.* — *Straight No Chaser Magazine*, 1997.

bad-minded: malicious, unsympathetic, or cynical.

> *Bad-minded, she had cussed. That had sent the chill right through.*
> — Diran Adebayo, *My Once Upon A Time*, 2000.

seen!: an exclamation said as an expression of approval or agreement, or when seeking confirmation of an utterance.

> *See it deh? ... believe you me, you will get far, jus' stay on the right track, seen!?* — Courttia Newland, *The Scholar: A West Side Story*, 1997

South African English

South Africa, the 'rainbow nation', is a complex country in terms of its linguistic heritage, which historically includes influences from Portuguese, Malay, Dutch/Afrikaans, the Khoi and San languages, both the Nguni and Sotho language families, and languages of South Asia. In 1994, the number of official languages grew from two to eleven, with English and Afrikaans sharing this status with nine regionally-based African languages. Although there are only 3 million first-language English speakers in a population of over 40 million people, English is the dominant language of business, education, and (since 1994) of government, and serves as the main medium of communication between the language-groups.

English has been established in South Africa since the early 19th century, and many English words have developed new meanings which are standard in the English spoken there.

These include **motivation** (a proposal with supporting arguments, for funding etc.), **circle** (a roundabout), and **robot** (a set of traffic lights). Coinings include **interleading** (interconnecting: used of rooms or doors), **frail care** (care for the infirm elderly), **chalkdown** (a teacher's strike), **frothy** (a fit of temper, a tizzy), and **yesterday, today, and tomorrow** (a flowering garden shrub).

The colloquial English of the new South Africa shows the influence – especially in vocabulary, but also occasionally in grammar – of the languages with which it interacts, particularly Afrikaans. The result is both colourful and unique.

indaba: a gathering or discussion. This word originally applied to a traditional tribal meeting, but is now used generically for any gathering. It is also used in the expression 'That's your indaba', meaning 'That's your problem'.

babalaas: a hangover, or (as an adjective) hung-over. From Zulu *ibhabhalazi*, via Afrikaans.

skop, skiet, en donder: used to describe a film, book, computer game, etc. that is characterized by violence. It derives from the Afrikaans for 'kick, shoot, and beat up'.

pondok: a shack or shanty-dwelling. Derived from Malay, 'shed, hut'.

braai: a barbecue. Derived from Afrikaans, 'grill'.

eina: the standard exclamation of pain. From Khoikhoi, via Afrikaans.

the bundu: the wild. Possibly derived from Shona *bundo* grasslands. To **bundu-bash** is to travel through wild terrain.

monkey's wedding: simultaneous rain and sunshine – the term is probably related to the Portuguese *casamento di raposa* meaning 'vixen's wedding', denoting the same.

23.

Sound and Fury: The Changing Pronunciation of British English

❝ At bottom, ways of speaking are first and foremost ways of sounding the way we think we should sound, given who we are. ❞

Deborah Tannen, Professor of Linguistics at Georgetown University, Washington

JUST AS THE PHRASE 'Standard English' can mean different things to different people, so in Britain there is much confusion over the term 'Received Pronunciation'. Many people see the two as being one and the same, and as representing the educated and 'correct' English spoken by the broadcast media and particularly the BBC.

In fact, logically, Standard English has many regional standards with different accents and patterns of pronunciation, a reflection simply of the diversity of its users in populations that have become increasingly mobile. Yet logic is often missing in discussions of pronunciation; it is an issue which can excite passionate views among the British, where the delusion can still persist that all educated people speak alike. In 1999, the novelist Beryl Bainbridge incurred the wrath of many when she suggested that all regional accents, and particularly the Scouse of her home city Liverpool, should be eradicated.

If Bainbridge seemed to be struggling for a London voice which may not exist, she is not alone. In Britain particularly the

history of discrimination on the basis of pronunciation is
a long one. A constant throughout the centuries has been the
power of London society to define the norm to which every
Briton must aspire. Tom McArthur, in his *Guide to World
English* (OUP, 2002), traces this influence as far back as to
the 16th century when 'the London elite had begun to regard
regional and lower-class accents as comic, quaint, inadequate,
and vulgar'. This belief that 'correct pronunciation' is defined by
London and the South of England can lead to significant
stereotyping. Sometimes just one phonological feature is taken
as confirmation that 'proper' English is dictated by the capital:
that, for example, people in Birmingham may pronounce *thing*
as *fing* is automatically seen as a result of Cockney English. In
reality it is a national change which has been around for decades
and which has never been reliant on London for its lead.

A London-centric view of pronunciation persists in the
phenomenon of 'Estuary English', a newly observed variety of
English pronunciation said to be spoken in London and around
the Thames estuary, and seen by young people as being up-
front and high on 'street cred'. Some dialectologists see Estuary
English as a phenomenon created entirely by the British media,
or simply an affectation: 'Somebody who went to a good
university has no excuse for speaking in that ghastly estuary
sludge', wrote Michael Henderson in the *Daily Telegraph*,
referring to the England cricket captain, Nasser Hussain.
Others say that Estuary English is simply a 'poshed-up' Cockney
English, or conversely the result of the 'dumbing-down' of
Received Pronunciation. Whatever its origins, most now agree
that the speech patterns it describes (*footbaw* for *football*, for
example, or the dropping of 't's) are far from limited to the
areas around the Thames Estuary – many were in evidence in
Northern England, for example, for a very long period before
the term hit the headlines – and so Estuary English, whatever
else it is, may be something of a misnomer.

In fact, education in the 21st century is more democratic
in respect of both gender and class, and southern England no
longer holds the grip on linguistic prestige which it had on
Britain a century ago. Over the last hundred years there has

been a steady reduction in the social distance between dialects and accents, thanks to the processes of urbanization and to the enormous increase in global forms of communication. Increasingly, pronunciation patterns are becoming less a matter of origin and more one of lifestyle choice. BBC English was once seen as a marker of education and authority; now it is more likely to be taken as a marker of out-of-touchness and snobbery. Conversely, regional accents are cherished as typifying honesty and openness. It is interesting today to compare the cut-glass diction in news items from the Second World War with the down-to-earth briefings (even if, as the papers noted, the spokespeople were all 'posh') from the 2003 Gulf War.

Pronunciation can be as powerful a marker of social identity as the latest slang, and young people in particular are adopting linguistic mannerisms which send out strong signals to others as to which group they belong. Adult pressures can be equally strong, with a neutral RP voice being the accent of choice in certain circumstances or professions, whilst the colour of selected regional accents (Edinburgh or the West Country, for example, but not Newcastle or Birmingham) is often preferred in others – including, interestingly, broadcasting.

Below are some examples of our changing voices, reflecting local and national influences but also some imported from further afield.

Glottal stopping

A glottal stop – the quick stopping of sound created when the flap of skin in the throat called the glottis closes the air flow so that, for example, *rotten party* is pronounced *ro'en par'y* – is a feature of particular accents rather than the result of sloppy speech. It is found both in Cockney English and in many regions of modern Britain including Scotland (and particularly Glasgow), where some say the glottal stop originated. It is not found in 'Received Pronunciation', which is why it is viewed by many as wrong. Today many people, and particularly the young, swallow their 't's in such words as *sta'ement* and *sea'belt*. Whilst the use within a word (whereby *water* becomes *wa'er*) is often still viewed as being Cockney, the glottal stop is also extending

to the final 't' in words: *quite easy* becomes *kwai easy*, and
take it off, *taik i off*.

'Th'

The shift in the pronunciation of 'th' in British English has
been significant, and many people now substitute 'f' as a
matter of course: *barf* (for *bath*), *mouf* or *muf* (for *mouth*)
and *enfusiasm* are their norm. This phenomenon of what
dialectologists call 'Th-fronting' can be traced as far back as the
mid-1860s and to Yorkshire, and is certainly on the increase
today.

In addition to this move towards a soft 'th' in the 'f' sound,
the use of a hard 'th', whereby it is pronounced as 'v', is also
spreading. The resulting delivery: *Wha's up wiv ya bruvver?*, is
as much a social distinction as one of regional pronunciation.

H-dropping

The letter 'h' at the beginning of a word is no longer pronounced
by many in Britain. ''*and on 'eart*' instead of *hand on heart* is a
good example. Now evident nationally, the dropping of 'h' was
traditionally a feature of the speech of the extreme north of
England as well as the Lake District, East Anglia, and a band of
the West Country. Again it is often used to mark out social
groups rather than regional heritage.

Changing sounds

Other individual pronunciation changes on the increase, whilst
not necessarily new, include:

milk pronounced as *miwk*, and *bottle* pronounced as *bottoo* or
bo'oo.
way pronounced as *why*, and *say* pronounced as *sigh*.
Tuesday becomes *choosday*, or even *toosday* in the American
(and Northern English) model.

fuhn/fun

An interesting trend in British pronunciation seems to be the
blurring of some previously hard distinctions between North

and South. So where *fuhn* (where the 'u' sound is as in *put*) and *fun* were the telltale signs of Northern or Southern origin respectively, many now adopt a pronunciation which sits slightly in the middle and which has a slightly, but not very, rounded 'u'.

right/wight

Convergence is also evident in the increasing tendency to use 'w' for 'r'. Previously regarded as an affectation by the upper classes but also a genuine feature of working-class speech, examples such as *wabbit* for *rabbit* are losing their class connections and becoming instead a marker of group identity among the young.

Talking up

He uptalks, my son. You've probably experienced it, like all the doctors and people who have studied it. I think it comes from kids who want to be heard, and they're afraid that if they stop, adults are going to cut them off. – Danny DeVito

A further development in the sounds of British English is the rise of what has been called 'uptalk' or 'upspeak': the use of a rising tone within a statement where a fall might be expected, so that it sounds like a question even when it isn't. The written equivalent is to put a question mark at the end of every sentence. No one can definitively pin down uptalk's geographical origins – the most popular theory is that the speech pattern started in Australia or California – and it may well have emerged in several different places more or less synchronously. What is not in doubt however is its spread within Britain, influenced to a large degree by television and particularly by Australian soaps such as *Neighbours* and American sit-coms such as *Friends*. Like 'Valspeak' or 'mallspeak', two features of West Coast language in the US, 'uptalk' is used to signal group identity among the young. It is also showing signs of receiving formal recognition: many English language teaching tapes use uptalk as an imitation of how English is spoken today. If you are a non-English speaker using the new generation of audio material, you will learn to speak uptalk.

24.

The Sound of American English

> ❝ Language does not consist of letters, but of sounds, and until this fact has been brought home to us our study of it will be little better than an exercise of memory. ❞
>
> *Archibald Henry Sayce, philologist, 1879*

Pronunciation is one of the most immediately obvious features of a region's linguistic identity. Like grammar and vocabulary, the sound of each dialect reflects historical facts of migration, social facts of ethnicity and geographical facts of terrain. Perhaps nowhere is the number and variety of influences at work within each of these categories greater than in the United States. Americans draw on the variations in accents as material for much of their comedy (the Southern drawl, the New York twang) in a way which suggests that differences in pronunciation within their country are as great as those across the Atlantic. That Southerners say *wah* for *why*, Bostonians *noath* for *north*, and (some) New Yorkers *gawuhlic* for *garlic*, would seem to suggest the same. It is all the more surprising, therefore, that there is such similarity in speech patterns across it, suggesting that there is some sort of 'average' pronunciation which its population unconsciously follows.

If such an average does exist, it is usually said to be that of General American, also known as Broadcast Standard. Derived from a generalized Midwestern accent, it was once the only way of speaking by newscasters, before the 1960s saw a decline in the popularity of the idea of a uniform accent across the country. The nearest equivalent to the Received Pronunciation of British English, Broadcast Standard is still regarded by some as a norm from which all other regional patterns diverge.

As elsewhere, television and mass media are powerful forces in standardizing American pronunciation and smoothing out regional differences, but they can also be instigators of change, serving as literal mouthpieces for new sounds. The young are particularly responsive to such innovations, and a view of pronunciation by age gives us a snapshot of change in progress: so *err* is pronounced as *air* rather than rhyming with *purr* as it used to, and *dour* now rhymes with *flour* rather than *poor*.

Below is a brief look at some of the other major patterns actively forming the phonetic landscape of the US.

The 'r' sound

The dropping of an 'r' sound after a vowel, and replacing it with another vowel, is becoming increasingly common. The shift, for example, from the 'r' to 'ah' as in *what a boah* or *it's over theah*, is something we associate with old movies and stars such as Katharine Hepburn. Its geographical origins are Eastern New England and parts of the South, particularly in states such as Louisiana and Alabama where 'plantation' culture once existed. Today it is also very much a part of Black English vernacular.

Historically this dropping of the 'r' sound has served as a signal of social class. Certainly in the early movies it had a high status and seemed to imitate British English (as it was). William Shetter, in his excellent *Language Miniature* study of the phenomenon in 2000, sees a gender difference too, noting that it was almost invariably the woman who had the higher-status, 'r-less' pronunciation, with the male leading role more often pronouncing the lower-status 'r'. What is interesting today is that its function looks to be reversing, so that the dropping of 'r' suggests a speaker of lower status. It is perhaps for this reason that New Yorkers, in whose speech the lack of 'r' was once a key feature of prestige pronunciation, are re-adopting the 'r' sound to avoid appearing vulgar. So *oil* and *earl*, the sounds of which often swapped over in New York speech, may revert back to their original pronunciations, and the classic example of *tuh-ee-tee tuh-eed* for thirty third will now be permanently confined to media parodies.

Labov's department stores

These differences between what is called an 'r-full' (and also the 'rhotic r') pronunciation, as in *New York*, and an 'r-less' pronunciation, as in *New Yawk*, were studied in the 1960s by the academic William Labov, who chose a novel and imaginative means of recording sound changes.

Labov visited three New York department stores, which traditionally served different social classes, to assess the difference in the pronunciation of 'r'. These were Saks, which he termed 'high prestige', Macy's, which was 'middle prestige', and lastly S. Klein – a 'low prestige' store. In each of these he asked various clerks for the location of an item he knew to be on the fourth floor. By evaluating their answers he could verify whether 'r' was indeed a strong indication of social status.

The results of the experiment showed that more clerks pronounced their 'r's in the higher-prestige store Saks than in either of the other two. Correspondingly, the most prominent 'r' dropping was in S. Klein. Within Macy's, Labov conducted a further experiment whereby he asked different levels of employee the same questions, again eliciting the answer 'fourth floor'. What he found was an even stronger pattern, with 46% of all 'floorwalkers' pronouncing their 'r's, and only 14% of store clerks pronouncing theirs.

cot/caught

A growing minority of US speakers do not distinguish between the sounds in such words as *cot/caught*, *collar/caller* and *Don/dawn*: in other words they lack or have less lip rounding when pronouncing words with a short 'o'. Once associated with Boston and the Eastern US, this shift is becoming noticeable nationally.

pin/pen

Another widespread merger of sounds is in the pronunciation of the vowel 'i' before the consonants 'n' and 'm': so *pen* sounds like *pin*, and *hem* like *him*. Long a characteristic of the speech of the Southern States, it now appears to be widespread through the South Midland area (southern Ohio, Indiana, Illinois, Missouri and Kansas), as well as in Texas and some areas in the West.

Generational changes

Linguists have long noted differences in pronunciation patterns according to gender and age. Younger American females today are said to be talking increasingly rapidly, dropping syllables and barely articulating consonants in the process: a result perhaps of the influence of 'Valspeak'. 'Uptalking', the form of speaking which adds an invisible question mark to every statement, is also a strong feature of the speech of the young, and its increasing evidence in Britain is thanks in no small measure to the influence of American culture.

25.

Fictional Realities: The Language of TV

❝ I believe the subtext here is rapidly becoming the text. ❞

Buffy the Vampire Slayer

NO ONE CAN DISPUTE the extraordinary influence of television in the last fifty years nor, more importantly, its power to transform. TV is undoubtedly one of the strongest forces behind language change. In 2003, the French Education Minister announced that French secondary-school children are to watch *EastEnders* to sharpen their language skills, prompting the snort 'Yer 'avin a larf, intcha?' from much of the British media. TV disseminates language, but it also creates it, and it is not always easy to tell the difference: whether a word was created by a scriptwriter or simply picked up and then broadcast to millions. Whichever it is, the most successful TV shows have become impressive forces in the lexicon of popular culture.

Today's TV hits often play consciously on the boundaries between fiction and reality. The fictional US President Jed Bartlet in *The West Wing*, the American political drama set in the White House, was the preferred choice of the American electorate when pitched in a virtual contest against George W. Bush. Bartlet hit the headlines again when the anti-war stance of the actor playing him, Martin Sheen, sent his popularity in the opposite direction. Was it Bartlet or Sheen being reviled? No one was quite sure, and when Tony Blair was reported to have asked one of *The West Wing*'s scriptwriters for advice on education and benefits policy – 'any minute now and we'll have

Rob Lowe called in for a Downing Street summit', said one backbench MP – political life was irrefutably imitating art. The series has received much acclaim for its witty and quick-fire dialogue, and one could argue over whether its scriptwriter Aaron Sorkin is taking his lexicon from political life, or contributing to it. One of the earliest episodes of *The West Wing* had the title 'Taking Out the Trash Day', named after the practice of slipping out unpopular news when there is already bad news in the headlines. This proved to be unwittingly prophetic of former political adviser Jo Moore's now notorious email to British government colleagues on 11 September 2001 – 'a good day', she wrote, 'to get out anything we want to bury'.

There are many more instances of television blurring the lines between the real and fictional worlds. When Tony Soprano of *The Sopranos* quoted from Sun Tzu's *The Art of War*, sales of the 2,500-year-old manifesto shot up. Meanwhile viewers today are exhorted to see celebrities as they are in 'real life' when plunged into the unreal surroundings of the jungle or held captive in a house. Perhaps the words from television which most penetrate daily life, however, are catchphrases. A catchphrase is a highly useful tool for a scriptwriter in that it becomes a distillation of the character speaking it. Jim Royle's 'my arse' (*The Royle Family*), Ali G's 'Respec', Homer Simpson's 'Doh', and Del Boy's 'luvvly jubbly' (*Only Fools and Horses*), all function in the same way, by becoming shorthand for the character and his or her personality traits – so much so sometimes that they eventually lose their connection with their originators and we begin to use them as standard phrases rather than in conscious quotation.

The Sopranos was one of a number of programmes – including *Sex and the City* and the reality TV show *The Osbournes* – which showed TV breaking language taboos. We have it to thank too for building on the knowledge of mobspeak first gained from James Ellroy and from Mario Puzo's *The Godfather*: for 'going to the mattresses' (going to war with a rival clan), 'skeevy' (to disgust), and 'goomah' (a Mafia mistress). And of course for 'Bada bing!', the name of the New Jersey strip-club featured in the series and now part of laddish idiom in the phrase 'bada bing bada boom'.

If *The Sopranos* picks up the dialects of Naples and Sicily, other television writing shows a desire to create new language. One of the most striking of these is the show *Buffy the Vampire Slayer*, which coins slang terms and phrases in almost every episode, both by combining familiar slang and making it into something new, or by real invention. Language is never irrelevant to its story. 'Slayer Slang', as it has become known, and explored by academics such as Michael Adams who has given us a whole lexicon of Buffy speak, gives us a particularly vivid snapshot of the preoccupations of American youth culture today. It also provides one of the most startling proofs that television both intrudes on and participates in language: a glance at the vocabulary of teen magazines, chat rooms, and web-sites suggests that Slayer Slang may well last longer than the (now-ended) programme that spawned it.

Here is a selection of examples from some of the TV shows currently influencing our language; there are many more.

Buffy the Vampire Slayer

Slayer Slang takes American Californian high-school 'Valspeak', created in the 80s and popularized in films such as *Clueless*, and pushes the envelope to make it vivid, inventive, and fun. The conscious play with language is explicit and an essential part of characterization. Many of the show's characters – and particularly Buffy herself – muse out loud about the role of language in their internal and external lives, and use words to often new and brilliant effect.

- I'm the very spirit of vexation. What's another word for 'gleaming'? It's a perfectly perfect word as far as many words go but the bother is nothing rhymes, you see. (Buffy)

- Doesn't Owen realize he's hitting a major backspace by hanging out with that loser? (Cordelia)

- Whatever is causing the Joan Collins 'tude, deal with it. Embrace the pain, spank your inner moppet, whatever, but get over it. (Cordelia, to a petulant Buffy)

A *Buffy* glossary

vague up: to make less clear.
Buffy: *Gee, can you vague that up for me?*

supporto: supportive, '*I'm supporto gal*'. The adjective ending '-o'
is particularly productive in *Buffy*, and is probably a development
from the word *mondo*, used in reference to something very
remarkable of its kind (e.g. *mondo weirdo*). Other trademark terms
include **bizarre** (weird), and **percepto** (perceptive).

five by five: perfect, fine.
Willow: *I'm wicked cool, I'm five by five.*
Tara: *Five by five? Five by five what?*
Willow: *See, that's the thing. No one knows.*

cuddle-monkey: a passionate or sexually attractive young man or
woman.
Xander: *Every woman in Sunnydale wants to make me her cuddle-
monkey.*

kicking the gear stick: having sex.
Faith: *Bet you and Scott have been up here kicking the gear stick …
Do you ever catch kids doing the diddy up here?*

mootville: irrelevant.

much: very, really, intensively, as in *pathetic much*, or in phrases
following the pattern 'how much the … [creepy]'.
Buffy: *How did he die?*
Cordelia: *I don't know.*
Buffy: *Well, are there any marks?*
Cordelia: *Morbid much? I didn't ask.*

A world of no!: definitely not.

Decafland: the calm realm between **Comaville** and **Speedtown**.

carbon-dated: very out of date.
Buffy: *Look at his jacket*
Giles: *It's dated?*
Buffy: *It's carbon-dated.*

jonesing: to have an urge or a need. The phrase is said to come from Jones Alley in Manhattan, associated with drug addicts. Buffy: *Oh boy, I was really jonesing for another heartbreaking sewer talk.*

Da Ali G Show

The notoriously politically incorrect persona of Ali G first came to attention on *The 11 o'Clock Show*. His influence in the space of a short time has been great: even the Queen Mother was said to have mimicked his catchphrase 'Respec!'. The creation of Sacha Baron Cohen, Ali G is is a white *gangsta* rapper wannabe (also known as a *wanksta*) who speaks a jumbled argot of cockney, Jamaican and hip-hop slang. The format of *Da Ali G Show* is based on interviews with usually unsuspecting subjects, their perplexed replies and bemusement in the face of outrageous questioning providing the comedy of the show.

The humour of Ali G looks likely to remain in Britain – a recent tour of the US left critics outraged and much of the American public unmoved, although it certainly resulted in some truly surreal interviews with major US political figures.

The Ali G lexicon

Ai!: Yes!

booyakasha!: all right!

keeping it real: rap term for telling it like it is, or being honest. Ali G often uses the term to express admiration for his interviewee.

ride the punani: hip-hop slang for having sex; *punani* is female genitalia in black slang, and was first popularized in Jamaican dance-hall reggae lyrics. It can also be used, as it is by Ali G himself, to describe good-looking and sexy women collectively.

all-dat: everything.

me main man: black American slang for 'my favourite person', and used by Ali to describe David Beckham. It has its female equivalent too: *Me main girl Madonna ere says it's cool.*

selecta: a late 1990s dance music term originally meaning a DJ, and used by Ali to denote pleasure or approval. He often precedes it with *bo*, as in *bo selecta*: *Selecta! I is ere wiv none uver dan de Queenie Mum of pop muzic, Madonna. Check it!*

racialist: term to describe anything from racist to something which is discriminatory. To Admiral Stansfield Turner, when hearing that CIA membership requires a college degree, Ali says: *Ain't that a bit racialist though that you have to be intelligent?*

hypcriticalist: hypocritical: *Ain't it 'hypcriticalist' that so many nuns work as strippers?*

Seinfeld

Seinfeld, seen by some as the most influential and successful US situation comedy of the 1990s (it finished in 1998), is a further example of a television show that uses language self-consciously. The absurd situations, the comedy, and the commentary are all remarkably language-based. Beyond the many catchphrases it indisputably generated during its eight-year run (the most famous of which is *yada yada yada*) can be heard a wealth of entirely new words, some of which have transcended their makers and are still in evidence five years on.

The co-writers of the series, and co-creator Larry David in particular, played with language in almost every episode. When a woman tells Jerry, who is pretending to be unfunny, that she thought he was happy-go-lucky, he replies 'I'm not happy and I'm not lucky. If anything I'm sad-stop-unlucky'. There is a clear delight in turning nouns into verbs – *bagel*, *dictator*, *Guggenheim*, *kibosh*, *spatula*, and *steel-toe* are all used as verbs in one or more *Seinfeld* episodes – and in creating new words by removing real or imagined parts of existing ones (such as *bobulate* below).

The following examples of 'Seinlanguage' demonstrate further categories of conscious and effective word-play.

bobulate: to be composed and level-headed (i.e. the opposite of *discombobulate*). Other examples of this type of word-play include **odorant** (from *deodorant*) and **perspirant** (from *anti-perspirant*).

playing with confederate money: having silicone breast implants.

going downtown: having sexual intercourse.

ghost read: to read a book for someone else (in the model of *ghost write*).

level-jumping: assuming a closer friendship than actually exists.

blow-off number: a wrong phone number given to an unwanted suitor.

must-lie situation: a situation in which lying is the only prudent course.

non-date personality: the (more natural) personality one exhibits when not on a date.

ribbon bully: a person who tries to force others to wear a ribbon which symbolizes a cause or charity.

hand sandwich: a handshake in which one person places their free hand over the the top of the other person's shaking hand.

regift: to give as a gift something that one has received as a gift oneself.

shushee: a person who is being shushed. The **Unshushables** are those *shushees* who refuse to stop talking.

LINGUISTIC SIGNATURES: WORDS ON THE SCREEN

Thousands of words have been created or regenerated by the power of television and film. The following terms and phrases have all starred on the small or big screen. Some have been invented for them.

babelicious: gorgeous. The term was first used in a *Saturday Night Live* sketch, and subsequently in the film *Wayne's World*.

dirty dancing: dancing to music in a sexy and provocative way. The term was popularized by Emile Ardolino's 1987 film of the same name.

full monty: the works; naked. The term itself dates back to at least the 80s but came back into currency in 1997 in the wake of the film *The Full Monty*.

goodfella: a gangster. The word became popular as a result of the film *Goodfellas*.

her indoors: 'the wife', famously used by the character Arthur Daley in the British series *Minder*.

hood: a neighbourhood in the inner-city, inhabited mainly by non-whites. This sense of the word originated in the 60s but became more popular as a result of the 1991 film *Boyz N the Hood*.

luvvly jubbly: this term of affirmation or delight originated as an advertising slogan in the fifties for the orange drink Jubbly, but was popularized in the 80s by the character Derek Trotter in the series *Only Fools and Horses*. It is now frequently used as an adjective and interjection for its connotations of the attitude and somewhat dishonest entrepreneurial activities of the South Londoner 'Del Boy'.

mook: an incompetent or stupid person. The term was around in the 1930s but was regenerated by the US film *Mean Streets* directed by Martin Scorsese.

poptastic: fantastic, from *The Harry Enfield Show*.

toast: a person or thing that is defunct or dead. The use of the word comes from the film *Ghostbusters* and was first used by the actor Bill Murray in the line 'this chick is toast'.

warp factor (also **warp speed**): from *Star Trek*.

26.

A Word a Year: 1903–2003

HOWEVER SHORT-LIVED, each new word leaves a footprint in its language's history. The following selection of words coined over the last hundred years provides a series of clues as to the preoccupations of their time. Singling out just one word for each year is of course misleading: hundreds of new words are being created at any one time, and, however ephemeral they turn out to be, almost all will tell a tale about their environment. Nonetheless a quick glance through the list gives a fairly accurate impression of the shifting concerns of the English-speaking world as the 20th century progressed and the 21st began.

Many words surprise with their earliness. We remember the *Desert Rats* of the Gulf War, without perhaps realizing that those who served in the UK's fabled 7th Armoured Brigade were heirs to a tradition started in North Africa in 1944. Other surprises might include *Chunnel* dating as far back as 1928, *snog* originating in the 1940s, and *burger* belonging to the 1930s. The dates given represent the year of the first printed record of the word in question, rather than the time when it made a convincing impact on the language. Some words can remain unobtrusive for years until they come to prominence through a particular event or social change. Slang too takes a while to filter through, although not many of us would perhaps have put the verb *to diss* as far back as the 1980s.

The journey from *gamma ray* to *SARS* does not seem like a hundred years. Perhaps what this list articulates best of all is the circularity of language, as well as its powerful adaptability to the changing needs of its speakers.

1903	gamma ray (electromagnetic radiation)
1904	telephone box
1905	hormone
1906	chicken run
1907	cornflake
1908	airliner
1909	aileron
1910	rummy (card game)
1911	floozy
1912	Alzheimer's disease
1913	talkies
1914	legalese
1915	cushy
1916	postmodernism
1917	Nissen hut
1918	umpteen
1919	Jerry (a German)
1920	T-shirt
1921	tear-jerker
1922	offbeat
1923	hi-jack
1924	Velociraptor (a fast-running, two-legged dinosaur.)
1925	superstar
1926	gimmick
1927	pavlova
1928	Chunnel
1929	penicillin
1930	Nazi
1931	microwave
1932	green belt
1933	dual carriageway
1934	evacuee
1935	ecosystem
1936	demo

1937	hobbit
1938	germ warfare
1939	burger
1940	googol (a fanciful name for ten raised to the hundredth power)
1941	apparatchik (a member of the Communist party in the USSR)
1942	napalm
1943	card-carrying
1944	Desert Rat
1945	snog
1946	space age
1947	apartheid
1948	bikini
1949	Newspeak (the name of the artificial language used for official communications in George Orwell's novel *Nineteen Eighty-Four*)
1950	ayatollah
1951	biopic
1952	pony-tail
1953	videotape
1954	discotheque
1955	tracksuit
1956	glitterati
1957	pop art
1958	autocue
1959	cruise missile
1960	neutron bomb
1961	game show
1962	trendy
1963	Dalek
1964	quasar
1965	spacewalk
1966	centrefold
1967	generation gap
1968	cellulite
1969	homophobia
1970	hot pants

1971	chairperson
1972	flexitime
1973	-gate (following the model of Watergate)
1974	baby boomer
1975	fractal (a mathematically conceived curve)
1976	CFC
1977	palimony
1978	pay-per-view
1979	bungee jumper
1980	dis; diss (to show disrespect for someone)
1981	wannabe
1982	yuppie
1983	bog-standard
1984	spin doctor
1985	gobsmacked
1986	glasnost
1987	eco-terrorism
1988	road rage
1989	velvet revolution (non-violent political revolution)
1990	World Wide Web
1991	babelicious
1992	ethnic cleansing
1993	home page
1994	Blairism
1995	ladette
1996	alcopop
1997	identity theft
1998	text message
1999	blog (a web log or diary)
2000	dimpled chad
2001	shoe bomber
2002	axis of evil
2003	SARS